12/00

Welcome home, stranger

Welcome home, stranger

— an account of multiple personalities —

MATTHEW DANIELS

RANDOM
HOUSE
NEW ZEALAND LTD

RANDOM HOUSE NEW ZEALAND LTD
(An imprint of the Random House Group)

18 Poland Road
Glenfield
Auckland 10
NEW ZEALAND

Sydney New York Toronto
London Auckland Johannesburg
and agencies throughout the world

First published 1997
© Matthew Daniels 1997
The moral rights of the Author have been asserted.

Cover illustration and design by Chris Watkins
Author photograph on front cover by David Clinton

Printed in Wellington by Wright and Carman (NZ) Ltd
ISBN 1 86941 312 1

CONTENTS

AUTHOR'S NOTE

W<small>RITING THIS ACCOUNT</small> of my many lives has been a lengthy process involving great amounts of time and deep thought. As this is a very personal recollection of events, including details of other people's lives outside my own, I'd like to publicly make known the following: the least of my intentions, during and after the writing of this book, is to cause my family any unnecessary harm or anguish.

Some painful moments have been recorded here and at times it has been necessary to be frank about those around me. However, it has been important that the focus of such a diverse narrative be my own perceptions, my own perspective. Therefore I stress once again, this is principally my own story — taken from a collective viewpoint of the many selves who secretly shared my day-to-day existence.

Special thanks go out to all family members who have encouraged and supported me during the evolutionary process of assembling this account. Particular recognition is given to my mother and sister Nicole who have both been very patient — often telephoning and getting my answering machine. Thanks, too, to my two therapists for their warmth, understanding and ready ear when I needed them most. Special appreciation is due to all my friends of the South Island Writers' Association, Julie Williamson, and my writers' critique group for their support; also my doctor, other friends and acquaintances too numerous to mention.

Finally, with relief, my appreciation to all the staff at Random House New Zealand — especially Harriet, of course; my partner Chris; Noel Virtue and Michael Yeomans; and not forgetting Naomi.

"Onward and out of the battle zone."

M<small>ATTHEW</small> D<small>ANIELS</small>
1 March 1997

This is a creative response to trauma . . .

— Ralph MA(Hons) Dip.Clin.Psych. MNZPsS ANZIM MNZCC Psych

Like coming home from a nazi concentration camp and there's some heavy shit ahead . . . you're fragmented, but I can help you . . .

— Ralph MA(Hons) CQSW MNZASW MNZPsS

For my partner Chris
and for Noel Virtue and Michael Yeomans
in the spirit of love and friendship

PROLOGUE

*T*HIS *THING CALLED* "My Life" is unable to be explained, is a distant star within the nothingness which is supposed to be my universe. I am living — but how? — where? — when? — and why?

The only proofs that I exist are vague recollections of past time. I have memories, like cinematic footage, that verify this body must surely be mine. Threads of light are filtering down to a dark recess, shining upon my face, and instantly I'm here: in Christchurch, New Zealand, Planet Earth.

Having now left that dark void of suspended animation to repossess my body, I catch a glimmer of the truth as it dawns on me: So, okay, if I'm intermittently slipping to and from that dark place, how then can I assume control over this body? What governs it while I'm absent?

Looking in the mirror, I can't help but think: My body's somewhat beefy, evidence that something is feeding me. And to society I appear normal enough — alive — however, confused, anxious! A cyclic seed of doubt resurfaces: Do I eat for myself? Dress myself? Get up each morning? Have friends and some form of social life?

Enter, overwhelming sensations of dread and fear.

The situation increasingly worsens: Time becomes an invisible measurement which has utterly no relevance to me. Numbers on the clock face are mere symbols. Months and weekly dates are just black figures printed on something called a calendar.

This sliver of reality I call "My Life" confirms that I am actually existing — between two opposing poles, each a point in that abstract dimension called Time. I'm aware of being able to inhabit both past and present.

Enter, a second state of ignorance: Flashes of *déjà vu* provide a rear-window view into another life unlike my own. Blinded to accepting its existence, I tell myself, I wasn't there, don't even socialise in that kind of company, and I'm damned sure these "friends" are strangers. Such hazy recall of an extra life beyond this one is steadily gaining a sense of deeper clarity. So now I begin to question my sanity. Am I seriously ill? Or is this all a cruel work of fiction, a figment of the imagination?

To complicate an already bizarre set of circumstances, unknown voices are talking to me, within my mind, whenever I'm released from that dark place. Gradually, over an indeterminable length of time, I'm almost able to grasp hold of those other voices, only to discover that "they" have thought processes of their own. I'm now listening to their personal concerns issuing from that darkness which I will later come to call "the abyss". Slowly I'm becoming aware that these voices and their distinctly individual thoughts actually belong to other selves who are leading separate lives from mine — yet in me, through me.

While failing to comprehend how, I know that these selves are tuned in to my own thought processes. They're beginning to respond to my fearful inner questions, providing answers. They're saying, — We are here! . . . — Don't you know who I am? . . . — He said that, not me! . . . and then comes the breakthrough when one voice introduces a name, — It's Terry. I won't let you forget my name now you know I exist.

From this moment of awakening onward, I'm faced with a new dilemma: Who can I talk to about this? Not my doctor. Not the hospital system where I've acquired the diagnosis of "Chronic Schizophrenia". Not my family who'll have cause to believe that I'm weirder, more eccentric or mentally ill than they'd ever guessed.

The decision I make is simple: I'll never tell another soul about these "people" as I'm now calling them. Soon I'll become an expert at editing my own speech because "their" words and mannerisms are intermingling with my own. I'll learn to be a white liar, afraid that these Others may be noticeable in public.

Ironically, what I am now revealing, within the pages of this book, are recollections of their appearances in public — of having sexual relationships, of writing short stories and novels — while I'm "asleep" within the dark place. They go to movie theatres, drink alcohol at parties I'd never have the courage to attend, and sometimes they sabotage the life I'm barely living. As their varied lives unfold I discover much more than I can cope with. I see that some of them were present in my childhood, that they share my memories along with their own.

While I vow to myself that I'll always deny their existence they continue to break out of my reclusive lifestyle. I resort, once more, to the myth that I'm mentally ill. A diagnosis of schizophrenia is a convenient method to escape this complex reality.

To such great depths I go in my efforts to hide their existence that I'm tripping myself up with contradictions. I'm saying "we", "they" and "him" when in contact with society, forgetting to disguise the presence of the Others within me. Friends begin asking, "What do you mean, we?" Embarrassed, I cover up, "We? Oops, I mean I!" Members of my family continue to regard me as "unwell" or "confused".

Unable to cope with the bouts of amnesia and the fear of further dividing into more selves, I finally seek help from a private psychologist.

THIS ACCOUNT YOU'RE about to read chronicles what I now understand to be a conglomeration of selves, commonly known and categorised as Multiple Personality Disorder. At the time of writing this, I am aware that the latest term of reference coined by psychologists is Dissociative Identity Disorder, or DID, but throughout this account I'll keep to the more widely recognised MPD tag.

The period covered within these pages is the eleven years which I've spent in therapy from age eighteen, centring on the years 1986 to 1990, with fragmented reflections of my childhood.

For narrative purposes it is necessary to combine both of my therapists into one character whom I've called "Ralph". To portray the two thera-pists as individual people will only add further complication to the telling of my story — also, a lot of the first five years with my initial therapist has grown sketchy in my mind.

I've chosen to narrate this book as Matthew Daniels because in 1990 I changed my surname by deed poll to make a distinct and permanent cut with the past. My original family name I've fictionalised as "Nankavelle" to spare family members any embarrassment.

o n e

A S FAR BACK as I can remember I've always been afraid of doors.
I've beaten on doors with clenched fists, struggled and kicked desperately for a door to remain open, even ajar — afraid of what is behind me.

Either open or closed terrifies me. Hell is standing before an open door. Fear is the chilling uncertainty of not knowing what lurks behind a closed door. Desperation comes from groping about in darkness, ignorant of the touch of thirty-eight jangling keys which slip from my hands.

Perhaps if I was to become invisible I could slip through wood and glass, to roam endless corridors, to seek out what lies before and behind each door.

Above each of the doors a clock ticks. How much time have I got until the alarm rings, deafening to my ears, for somebody to self-destruct? And what does he or she become? A disintegrating mound of bubbling flesh, tearing and scratching at the hand of one who snatches up the book of survival?

1986. I'M EIGHTEEN years old, afraid of suburbia because it reminds me of home where I once belonged.

A light summer breeze blows the net curtains aside at the white painted window sill in my room. The time is somewhere after 2 am. I'm asleep but also awake, drifting upon the tide that flows between two opposing shores, weightless, my breath rising and falling, caught on a reef where I can easily be anchored to another dream.

I have fallen into a vortex. The kind of nightmare where one longs to scream but is betrayed by the body, paralysed, trapped within the cinema of the mind. I'm surrounded by a circle of doors, and stepping away from the centre where I stand, I walk over to a door and cross the threshold. Something unknown to me begins to approach. My heart palpitates. I sprint as fast as I can around the outside of the circle of doors. I hurriedly choose another door and turn the steel handle. From here I run, a blur in flight, in and out of the circle, opening and closing many doors as I go.

I feel like a mouse in a spinning wheel. Who or what is chasing me? I pause in the centre of the circle for a moment when suddenly a cloak of black anxiety descends from a non-existent sky. It clings to my body like a second skin, leprosy, a poison coating of fate. Now I'm the master of myself. The thunder of reality splits through my mind. I realise that what is chasing me . . . is me! From the circle's centre I scream, "Let me out!" Running around to each door, I beat my fists upon them but none will open. Have I trapped myself? Let me out!

— Why should I let you go? demands a disembodied voice.

"Let me out! Who are you?" I cry, wanting freedom.

Laughter echoes from the circle of locked doors. I tell myself that this is only a bad dream, that I will awaken soon, the sun will shine through my net curtains and morning will have arrived.

— Don't you know who I am? questions the voice, sarcastic, a mouthful of bitter aloe. — Son of Sorrows. I know who you are!

I groan, sitting up in bed and reaching for a cigarette. My head throbs. "Phew, what a dream," I say aloud as if to comfort myself. But the dream hasn't ended yet.

— Nankavelle, I hate you!

Surely I'm going mad? Is it possible for characters to step out of dreams and enter into three dimensional reality? I feel the presence within my body. Son of Sorrows snatches the cigarette from my fingers and proceeds to smoke the low-tar filtertip. The hair on the back of my neck prickles.

— Go ahead, you idiot! Believe that I'm the product of psychosis! This is my body too.

I'm speechless. Even worse, I'm confused. Did I stub the cigarette out on the bedside cabinet? Come to think of it, I only recall lighting the damn thing! My head hurts. I feel drowsy, but as I lie down and drift back into sleep the stranger's voice comes into my mind again.

— Mind you don't set the house on fire! Shouldn't smoke in bed, he taunts, and like an unfocused camera shot, an image of an angry young man's face comes into my mind.

I'm crazy. This isn't real, I think, aware of the faint twitter of sparrows stirring in the trees outside my window.

"WHAT TIME IS it?" I yawn, rubbing both eyes which feel like pools of quicksand. My head still throbs.

"Eleven thirty," says my landlady. .

"What?" I jump out of bed feeling as if I've been hit by a train.

I take a sip of the overly sweet tea and walk over to the bench where I dial Doctor Weste's telephone number. "Hello, doctor . . . yes, I overslept . . . no, I don't feel well . . . I have a terrible headache . . ."

Before I can finish the sentence intense pain, a bolt of lightning, explodes within my head. Suddenly I've begun to fade. It feels as if I'm getting smaller, all the life siphoned out of me. Somebody stands before me in my mind. I'm blocked out, imprisoned by a dark recess, divided by a thin wall. What's going on? Hearing my own voice inside my head frightens me because I seem to be insignificant. Now somebody else, a second photographic negative, has become double-exposed over my soul. What the hell . . .? I ask myself, and I am overawed to hear a different voice coming from me: "And who am I speaking to?" this feminine voice breathes into the telephone.

But I manage to break out of the darkness into which I'm slowly descending. "Doctor," I say. "The blackouts are occurring more often!"

I'm about to recede into a black abyss of nothingness when I hear *her* voice again: "Thank you. But I don't need to see you, doctor. Goodbye."

The receiver is placed down. As suddenly as she appeared, she has gone. I'm left standing at the bench wondering what the hell is going on inside my head. How is it possible that I can spiral downward into the abyss of the soul, at the same time hearing and feeling the presence of another?

My God, I am thinking, I felt her separateness, quite distinctly. She is made of flesh and bone like me. She seems so utterly real. But what are these blackouts? How is it possible I can be in the shower on a Monday morning and then "snap to" only to find myself travelling across town on a bus on a Wednesday afternoon? What happens in between? Where have I been in the meantime?

I LOATHE THE set of old steel-weighted scales in the GP's musty office. Why can't Doctor Weste buy a set of electronic scales?

"Open your mouth," the doctor says, glasses perched on the end of his bulbous nose.

"Aaargh," I retch as my tongue is pushed aside by a wooden spatula.

"Good. Stand on the scales. Mmm . . . a little overweight. Okay, you can take a seat now."

Sitting at an ancient wooden desk, the doctor folds his arms together as if he were about to deliver a sermon. He's wearing the same woollen suit he's worn for the two years I've known him. He peers over the top of his glasses and begins a lengthy monologue about my health, how well I'm progressing — and Melleril!

"What!" I disagree. "Doctor, I feel nauseous. What about these headaches?"

He speaks to me as if I were a child, apple blossom in his tone. "Now now, my little rosebud. You have the Melleril twice daily and take nice walks around the river." He smiles like a saint.

What can I possibly say to him at this moment? I've often complained of headaches and mental blackouts. Now Doctor Weste has prescribed anti-psychotic medication. I leave the clinic feeling confused and walk into the local chemist. The pharmacist smiles politely as I hand a prescription over the counter.

The voice of Son of Sorrows thunders through my head.

— Will you look at that fucking smile! Bet the pharmacist thinks you're a schizophrenic. You idiot, Nankavelle. You let that doctor prescribe Melleril. Fuck you, Nankavelle!

I'm strongly aware that Son of Sorrows is now standing in my body and is staring hatefully at the pharmacist. I'm sick with guilt because I've been going to the pharmacist for many years. I attempt to smile at him.

— Why that damned smile on your stinking face, Nankavelle?

I wonder if my head is going to explode as I turn to the pharmacist. "Excuse me," I say, "can I have some water and two aspirin from the prescription?"

"Yeah. Won't be a minute," the man nods, heading to the back of the shop. I hear a tap running. I browse along the wall-to-wall shelving, trying on sunglasses, looking at homeopathic remedies, wanting a cigarette. I'm a caged animal. The other person inside is driving me crazy. I want to cry, feel utterly confused. I could easily quit on life. My right hand tingles as it is touched by the left hand. A chalk line has been drawn across my mind. I am again divided . . . two halves.

— Don't worry, Nankavelle. We'll be fine. We can get through this.

— What? I ask internally, feeling weary. I'm afraid of falling into the black abyss.

— We'll be fine, the soft voice repeats reassuringly.

— Who are YOU? I ask and my heart rate increases. Do I laugh and pass this off as another momentary lapse into madness? Should I cry? Perhaps I'll scream and this new voice will leave my mind, shoot out of my ears like a comet and never return?

— I'm Fourteen.

— Fourteen? How can you be fourteen?

— That's my name.

Oh, this is too much! I'm reeling, and hurry out of the chemist. I turn the corner into River Road and try to think about other things besides Son of Sorrows, the Woman, and Fourteen. I note how warmly the sun shines and wonder what it would be like to swim in the Avon River.

"Mr Nankavelle! Mr Nankavelle!" a voice calls from behind me. I turn around and look further up the road. The pharmacist is waving a green paper bag about. "You forgot your medication!" He walks up to me and, patting my shoulder, smiles. "Bit vacant today, aren't you? Must be the weather."

I force a smile. "Thank you."

As soon as I've spoken, Son of Sorrows rages inside me.

— A bit vacant? Nankavelle, you always were fucking vacant. Airhead!

— Leave him alone, whispers Fourteen. He has a headache.

I wish to God these others *would* leave me alone. I feel possessed, undermined again. I wave to the pharmacist before continuing along the road, watching the sunlight glimmer on the water. Bright rays of light reflect off the surface and stab into my eyes like slivers of glass. My head throbs.

t w o

AUDREY PAINTS HER nails. She has long bony fingers and each is splayed out upon the rickety wooden table. I think of chicken feet.
— Watch out, Nankavelle, you'll get henpecked!

"Oh, shut up," I say, standing up from my chair and pacing the dining room.

"There's no need to be rude," Audrey snaps. Her green eyes cloud over and her tight little mouth stretches into an O-shape highlighting her long ivory teeth.

"No, no," I exclaim, seating myself again. "I wasn't telling you to shut up. I was . . ." I fumble for words, deviate away from the truth and then snap back to reality like a rubberband. "I was telling a voice inside my head to shut up."

Audrey blows upon each nail. "Hmmm," she says, grinning, "that's okay. Just don't ever tell me to shut up."

"Yeah, right," I chuckle, downing a mouthful of hot tea while my face reddens. I'm embarrassed, wishing that I hadn't referred to the voices inside my head. God, she must think I'm crazy.

— Huh! You can't shut your stinking mouth for two minutes. Eh, Nankavelle!

This time I attempt to ignore his voice, hopefully block it out, but after a moment of deadly silence I bounce a thought back to Son of Sorrows in defence of myself: You wretched product of my imagination! Go back to the subconscious where you belong.

My head begins to throb. I close my eyes for a moment just as Audrey is about to deliver a lecture.

"Of course you're hearing voices. You don't get enough sleep, Matthew. You bang away on that old typewriter till all hours of the night, making a lot of noise. Anyway, what are you writing about?"

"What?" I ask, giving her a stupefied look. "Me? Writing? At night? You must be joking, Audrey."

"Don't play dumb with me." She stares at me and her thin, high eyebrows break into a frown. She drags on a cigarette, and after blowing a jet of smoke into the air, continues, "I hear you rip that damned paper out of the typewriter and thump your fist down on the table. You bang about in the kitchen. Taps turning on and off. The bloody jug boiling. All the noise keeps me awake half the night!"

I can't accept what I'm hearing. Is this some ploy to get me thrown out of the house?

— She's only the fucking landlady. You idiot, Nankavelle. If she doesn't like my late hours . . . ah, screw her! We'll live elsewhere.

I have to be diplomatic now to save my hide. Somehow I have to reason with Audrey, invent an excuse for why I'm up late at night, explain the activity. Trouble is, what can I give as a temporary reason until I can find out what my unconscious body is doing?

As I'm sitting there brooding across the table from Audrey, a little white lie, attractively packaged and gold wrapped, comes into my mind. The voice of Fourteen is soft, innocent:

— Tell the landlady you were restless on the nights Son of Sorrows was awake.

Ha! That's it! So it is Son of Sorrows who's been typing late at night. My anger toward him is justifiable now. Wait a minute: my psyche has somehow created this person, so can't it also erase him?

I feel a resistant force tearing around in my head. Fourteen is now shouting:

— Leave me alone!

— Bitch! Bitch! That little bitch has a big mouth, Nankavelle. I wouldn't listen to her if I were you.

The sobs of Fourteen reach a high pitch. I feel nauseous and vacate the chair, swing open the dining room door and run along the hall to the bathroom where I am violently sick.

"You alright?" calls Audrey.

"Just a headache. I might go back to bed for an hour or so."

By now Audrey is standing outside the closed bathroom door. "I don't mean to hassle you about being up late at night, but can you be a little quieter next time?"

I cup my hands under the cold water tap and, lifting them to my mouth, I drink the refreshing ice-cold water. The bathroom reeks of talcum powder and cheap apple shampoo. The hot water tap leaks slowly into the water-stained bath. Audrey knocks on the door.

"It's quiet in there. You okay, Matthew?"

"Fine," I say, flushing the loo before tipping Pine-O-Cleen into it. I now stand before the cabinet mirror. "You look like shit, kiddo," I laugh to myself. A sharp bolt of pain rages inside my head and in the dark misty haze of my mind I hear his voice again.

— You are shit, kiddo!

Audrey has gone back to the kitchen. "Can I get you anything?" she calls down the hallway.

"No," I groan, holding my head in both hands so that it doesn't topple off my shoulders. I head for my bedroom where I close the curtains and burrow into the cool creases of my unmatching bedsheets.

I AM VAGUELY aware of the door to my bedroom opening. I choose not to see who is entering the room. I can't be bothered now. I don't want to be torn from the sleep into which I'm descending. The bed begins to shake. Earthquake? Truck passing by the house?

"Wake up, you lazy shit!" She climbs onto my bed and proceeds to bounce up and down. "Come on, wake up! You haven't forgotten this evening?"

"Oh, Ugly-Bug. How could I forget? But I have an awful headache," I moan as she hands me a cigarette. The inside of my skull is like a football stadium. Balls are being kicked around, bounce, bounce. Noise. Feet booting my head in.

"You'll be fine. I'll introduce you to Vernon," she laughs, adding, "Selina and Jasmine are looking forward to seeing you."

"Ugly-Bug . . ." I yawn, staring at the digital clock which reads 4.12 pm.

"What?" she asks, taking the cigarette from my fingers.

"Firstly, who's Vernon? Secondly, fuck off!"

"Aw, don't be like that. See you at my house in half an hour," she pleads before grasping hold of the duvet and tearing it away from my body.

"Bitch! I'll be there in twenty minutes. You got any aspirin?" I rub my forehead. "Where are we going tonight?"

"The Millhouse. It's a rough place," she states, smiling wickedly at me.

She now bends over by the open door and farts. She breaks into laughter while I roll about on the bed laughing too.

"Ugly-Bug?"

"What?"

"You better have aspirin at your house!"

We are laughing so loud and with such reckless vehemence that I have to hold my head with both hands.

"What would your husband say if I told him you were bouncing up and down on my bed?" I grin widely, testing her out with this mock threat.

Ugly-Bug laughs. She looks like a blonde-haired golliwog. Her piercing green eyes search my face very carefully. She cackles, "He'd say that I'm a fucking mad bitch."

"You *are* a mad bitch," I howl, turning over on my stomach with my face into the pillow. "Go home. I'll be there shortly."

I hear the front door slam. I note a sound in the distance of Audrey baking something. The smell of raisins and rising dough wafts through my open bedroom door. I reach for a cigarette. Vernon? Who the hell is Vernon? Selina or Jasmine must be dating him.

THE ASPIRIN HAS worked, though now I feel depressed. I try not to let these grim feelings of muddy grey spoil the beginning of this evening.

Selina and Jasmine strut confidently into the Millhouses's crowded foyer with Ugly-Bug and myself trailing behind them. Three ugly-looking skinheads and a fat woman with no front teeth and greasy hair hover around the foyer. One of the skinheads lights a match as the fat woman lifts the joint to her mouth. A thick cloud of cannabis smoke clots up the atmosphere around the open door.

Ugly-Bug looks hatefully at the fat woman. The skinheads' eyes are glazed slits from an obviously high state of mind, and they stare blankly out the door.

I FEEL THE presence of Son of Sorrows. A sensation of cold ice slithers angrily through my veins. I'm wearing the black veil of hatred. It then occurs to me that Son of Sorrows has been glaring at one of the skin-heads. I turn to look at the interior of the pub now. I'm as sick and flimsy as a palm tree bracing against the full force of a tropical storm.

Why? I ask myself, but I can't answer that question. I'm passively aiming it at Son of Sorrows. I fear his rage. I fear the potential disasters that such a rage could bring upon me. Now it seems that my thoughts aren't private because Son of Sorrows has heard them and is replying:

— Why? Why! The reason I hate bald-headed pigs like those morons is because they violate any person who comes their way.

— So? I ask.

— You idiot. They are evil. Swastikas, Hitler, kill niggers, beat, kick, smash. Get the picture?

— Sort of . . . (I'm ashamed of such blind social intolerance.) How can I be so green?

Son of Sorrows rages on inside my head, — Green? You're more than naïve. You are so thick, Nankavelle. Keep away from those pigs. They are mindless, evil bastards.

I have to ask, for curiosity is getting the better of me: — But why? Many people do awful things in life. What makes them so different?

His voice is like thunder. His hatred chills me. — Don't ask me!

I push the issue now. — Why?

Son of Sorrows curses me in a final reply. — You are full of secrets! And as soon as this is said he has gone.

I'M AWARE THAT I've been seated at a table to the right of the bar for some time now. A glass of beer froths over in front of me. I hate beer! A lean handsome man in his mid twenties is shaking my hand.

"This is Matthew," says Ugly-Bug, introducing me to Vernon. Selina and Jasmine are on the opposite side of the crudely scoured table. My head is swimming.

"Hi," I mutter, feeling confused. Why has time taken me in an amnesiac state from the entrance door and seated me here? What have I been doing for the last few minutes? All at once I'm bewildered at the very concept of time itself. Panic surges upward from the pit of my stomach.

— Relax, says a new voice in an affected tone. You don't need to be afraid. . . .

Before I can begin to even grasp hold of what is happening inside myself, I start to fade. I'm descending into a dark space, sucked downward.

— Relax, says the voice again. You can rest now. Don't mind if I use your name?

Too late, I'm gone. Far away. Imprisoned in darkness where I can't feel anything except for the sound of myself breathing peacefully. I'm too astonished by this internal phenomenon to fight for my own resurfacing. I'm also too overwhelmed by the knowledge of another self to be bothered vying for time in the outwardly real, conscious world.

This is who I have become — dare I say, the impostor who's stolen the following moments from my life:

RUSSELL TAKES HOLD of my tall beer glass and drinks it slowly. He turns to Vernon and asks, "What's your favourite beer? I like Lion. Do they drink Lion in the army, soldier?" He's looking closely at Vernon, studying him, taking in the expanse of muscle and blonde hair. But before Vernon can speak, Russell is saying, "At ease, soldier!"

Vernon laughs. He's amused by this sudden attention.

Hmmm, this man has never met somebody like me. Mmm, this is going to be fun.

Selina and Jasmine are observing their soldier friend. Ugly-Bug rats around in her handbag for a cigarette. After retrieving a pack of B & H she lights the strong filtertip and blows smoke in Russell's face. Russell laughs confidently. He's going in for the kill.

"So, Vernon, what's it like being in the army?" He gazes intently into the soldier's face and at the same time reaches for a cigarette.

Vernon immediately pulls a lighter from his pocket. He says, "Being a soldier's great!"

"Mmmm." Russell places the filtertip in his mouth and the soldier goes to light it.

Ugly-Bug eyes the situation carefully and Russell notes that the soldier is looking cautiously at her. Their eyes meet and as this occurs, the others — including Russell — erupt into a wave of laughter.

Russell decides to make light of this moment. He slams the beer glass down upon the table and, looking directly into the soldier's eyes, exclaims, "Vernon, the girls here think I'm infatuated with you."

The soldier laughs.

"Actually, Vernon, they're right. So if this bothers you, well for godsakes at least have a beer with me before you slug me." He smiles, all the while laughing, and offers the soldier a cigarette. Vernon accepts it and his eyes glimmer.

This is a challenge. What beautiful eyes. The uniform! Phew, this is lust.

"Tell me," says the soldier, "what it's like."

Russell rolls his eyes as if he's having an orgasm. "Oh, you mean IT?" He's smiling a wicked mouthful of white teeth. For a moment he's deep in thought. Now he puts one hand to his mouth as if to suppress some intimate comedy playing inside his mind. He continues, "Well, what's IT like for you?" A statement, a test — stretch the elastic band, one foot in the end of a deep blue pool.

Vernon laughs. "I don't know. I haven't done IT your way before!"

Russell is revelling in the danger of this situation. "Well, there isn't much to IT." He decides to plunge deeper into warmer water. "Hey, soldier, what's it like wearing that uniform?" His eyes mist over.

The soldier chuckles. "My uniform? It's standard army issue. Yeah, I'm okay about wearing it."

"Really? Well, why don't you take it off?" He pours the soldier a beer. Ugly-Bug holds out a glass while Selina and Jasmine giggle.

Vernon stares at Russell a moment and, smiling, he says, "I like you!"

"Fascinating, aren't I?" Russell now passes the soldier a bowl of salted peanuts.

Vernon blows a stream of smoke into the air. "Seriously, I like you. Tell me about being gay."

Is this guy for real?

"Come up to the bar. I want to buy you a drink," Vernon offers politely.

As they veer toward the bar the girls leave the table and make for the dance floor. The barman fills two plastic jugs. He stares at Russell for a moment. "How old are you, kid?"

"Twenty."

"Bullshit. If the cops come in, you clear off — hear me!" He thumps the beer down on the bartop.

Ah, bugger him. I *am* twenty!

Seated back at the table, Russell and the soldier talk about many things. Vernon sheepishly admits that he is fascinated by Russell — who he is, what makes him gay. Naturally, Russell dispels all the myths: AIDS as a gay disease, husband-stealing, molesting twelve-year-old boys.

"Sheee-it!" sympathises the soldier." You put up with all that bigotry?"

"Yep," agrees Russell though he intends it to be a statement.

Ugly-Bug and the girls return to the table, and a short time later the closing call is announced.

"How are you getting home?" asks Vernon.

"Ugly-Bug is going to give me a lift. Nice to meet you, soldier. And don't take any notice of me teasing you about the uniform." Russell extends a hand.

Vernon laughs. "I'll give you a lift, Matthew."

"No thanks. Ugly-Bug doesn't mind driving me." He looks embarrassed now because Selina and Ugly-Bug are urging him to go with the soldier.

THE TAXI EASES into the petrol station. The driver pulls a plastic card from his wallet and heads for the attendant's counter. Russell and Vernon are in the back seat. Russell turns to the soldier and reaches forward to look into his face. For a brief moment they kiss.

I can't believe that I'm doing this!

Russell gazes at the soldier for a split second and then descends into the abyss of rapidly enveloping darkness within himself.

There follows a long silence.

I find myself seated beside a man in a khaki uniform, a stranger to me, and I'm knotted up with anxiety. I stare out the taxi window wondering, Where the hell have I been? Dark streets flash past the window. Somehow I have surfaced again.

I SLAM THE taxi door as I get out.

"See you again, Matthew." The soldier smiles warmly at me as he winds up the window. He knows my name. Who is he? I walk up the narrow pathway and knock on the front door. Audrey peers through the dining room curtains and I hear her pad toward the door. The affected voice of Russell speaks inside my head

— Sorry, I had to use your name.

"How was your night out?" Audrey asks, motioning with a wave of her hand for me to come inside.

"I don't know. I'm off to bed. Good night." I stumble along the hall and shut the bedroom door behind me.

Sleep doesn't come. I'm still wide awake at a quarter to five in the morning. Headaches. Blackouts. Confusion. People talking inside my head. I'm going crazy! Silently I weep into the pillow and pray an "Our Father". I drift into a long sleep soon after hearing the sparrows twittering outside my window.

t h r e e

"LET'S GO DOWN the river," the kids in my street used to say.

That was nineteen years ago. I still visit that place in my heart. It's all a blurred memory now but the taste of recollection lingers. I swear to God I can never completely forget the river, its sand, mud, green grassy banks overlooking mangrove-infested tidal flats.

The river is sacred. I remember fishing and swimming on its salty shores — I was innocent then like all the other childhood friends I had. East Tamaki, river of tainted water, I can never allow myself to forget you.

My dear Maori friend, Tau Paki, one year younger than me, aged nine, often bunked school to fish on the grassy bank which surrounds the mud-flat. I met him there, having stolen fresh slices of bread from the kitchen cupboard. I'd wrapped the thick slices in an old paper bag. Later on, Dad would discover that three smokes were missing from his pack — and yes, I'd borrowed his fishing knife, a nylon hand line, and the gaff. By four o'clock these items would have been discreetly put back in the old aluminium dinghy.

Tau looked up from his possie on a flat rock, his bare brown feet covered in thick grey mud. "Eh, Nannygoat, you wanker. What the fuck are you doing here?"

"Same as you." I was grinning from ear to ear and sat myself on a jagged rock beside my friend. My arse hurt but such an uncomfortable rock couldn't spoil a good afternoon's fishing.

"Shit, Nannygoat, you got a smoke?"

I pulled out two battered Pall Mall plains from my jacket pocket, straightened them out and offered my friend one. "Here," I said and Tau handed me the matches.

"Cool!" He spat into the water. We lit our smokes and as I daydreamed for a moment, Tau sliced up a worm and baited his line. I watched the line plop into the muddy water, the lead sinker causing a circle of rippling waves. I stopped daydreaming and baited my own hook, then, pulling a slice of bread from the bag, I laughed, "Geez, I'm bloody starving."

"Fuckin' worms in your gut? Eh, your arse, Nannygoat!" He tightened his jaw, rubbed his nose on his sleeve before reaching over me to retrieve a slice of bread.

"Worms? You black-arsed shit — more like shit in your taringas!" I knew my usage of the languages, Maori and English, really made him laugh.

We sat in silence and again my mind wandered. A scenario: the School Truant Officer catching us fishing, a lecture, and back to school, disappointed parents banging our ears . . . My attention to internal detail was interrupted by the sight of a steady stream of small air bubbles in the salty water about a foot in front of us. "Hey, Paki. Down there — look." I'd only just pointed to these when Tau abandoned his line, shoved the spool into my hand and crouched on the rock. He then tore up small portions of bread and dropped them into the water. "Cool!" I chimed. "Paki, you shit, you've got bites on the line."

My friend was absorbed by curiosity. He'd taken hold of my line, rebaited it, and was leaning over the rock, easing the line into the air bubbles. What followed was a flurry of mud, clouding up the water in streaks of dull colour away from the rocks. Tau was angry, his brown eyes narrowed, his chubby cheeks flushed. "Stinking shit of an eel!" he said, bending low into the crevasse of rock, clasping a fistful of small stones to throw them into the water.

I was laughing now.

"Don't laugh, you honky shit." Mischief glimmered in his eyes.

"Hey, black-arse, givvus a drag on that smoke before you ditch it."

He spat about an inch in front of my feet and handed me the cigarette. "Swim?"

"Yeah, alright." I wound the line around the plastic spool.

TAKING A SHORT cut around the mudflat, we hurried across the lawned boundary of a large modern house. An umbrella flapped in the breeze, turning occasionally from where it was planted through the centre of an iron barbecue table. A middle aged woman appeared from behind an oak door. "Oi, you kids, this is private property. Get off my lawn."

Moments later a bald-headed man stepped out from behind the woman. He crossed the well-cropped lawn, making an angry beeline our way. "Bloody kids! Why aren't you at school?"

We acted as if we were deaf. Our necks prickled with tension. We ran until the man was out of sight, laughing between ourselves. Out of danger, I asked Tau if he'd seen Murray lately.

"Eh, nah. Haven't seen him — but Chantelle's got the hots for him." He laughed, inserting one finger into his clenched hand to mimic sexual intercourse, making all the appropriate noises.

My mind, well educated in the school of life, clicked into overdrive and I elaborated on the facts of life. I mocked love and loving, saying, "Ah, must be love at first sight!" while my mind said, *Fucking*.

"Eh, Murray — the horny old bastard. And she's hot!"

Our discussion heated up as we laughed over what Murray might be doing with our nextdoor neighbour. Both Tau and I were too cocky to admit that our preoccupation with Chantelle was because our hormones were raging at the mere thought of her peeling a T-shirt away from her big Raquel Welch tits.

We were in for a surprise. Moored further along the river at a small wooden jetty was Murray's launch. A man we failed to recognise was painting around the window frames of the ancient boat. We stood on the jetty and watched him. A long time passed as, leaning over the steel railing, we shared the last cigarette.

The man on the launch adjusted a yellow sun-visor cap. Looking us over, he grinned, "You boys here to swim?"

Tau deflected the question by asking, "Where's Murray?"— and spat into the river.

"You know him?"

"Eh, that's his boat," my friend answered. His body language seemed to say, You think I was born yesterday? He liked to mock the older generation.

"Yeah, this is his boat." The man put down his paint brush. He seemed amused. "Shouldn't you two be at school?"

I glanced at Tau and rolled my eyes. I puffed on the cigarette and passed it back to my friend.

"School?" he mocked, making a thumbs-down sign. "Teachers are fuckin' wankers anyway."

"Just like Watson, eh?" I said.

"Eh, old baldy. Kinna help yah!" Tau laughed, rubbing an imaginary shiny bald head like Mr Watson's, our old teacher at Panama Road school.

The moment had gone. Tau was serious now: "Nannygoat. Betcha can't make it to that." He pointed out at the water.

I looked to the centre of the river. A strong current was pulling an unidentifiable mound of household rubbish toward the Howick bridge. I stared at the pylon out in the choppy water. "Swim to that? No way."

"Eh, chicken, eh?" He thumped my arm.

"Shit arse," I teased. I'd seen the *Jaws* movie. There was no chance at all that I'd swim out in that cold water, even if it meant proving myself to be tough.

We hung about for a while longer and when the old man stopped painting and went below deck we left the jetty. We decided to look for eels in fresh exposed mud and shallow water as the tide was going out.

TAU WAS ON his knees, hammering away at the hard earth on his mother's sloping front lawn. He was using a heavy rock and sharp stick because he wasn't allowed to play with the tools in the shed. His brow was beaded with perspiration, chubby cheeks flushing deeply.

"Hey, Paki, you got the matches?" I'd had my round at digging the earth and instead broke up fresh twigs for kindling. We lit the fire and stood back as it burnt down, thick grey smoke stinging our eyes.

His older sister Hine appeared in the front doorway. She called behind her, "Ooh, Mummy, Tau and Nannygoat got the matches . . ."

"Eh, Hine, you fat bitch — fuckin' tell on me!"

"Ooh, Mummy, he's swearing."

Seconds later Aunty Rona banged on the open window. "Boy, I'll slap your ears! Whatchoo doing out there? Ooh, you swear like that again and I'll wash your mouth out with soap! You hear me? . . . Tau?"

Hine closed the door. We could hear her in the front room saying to Aunty Rona, "Mummy, they playing with fire. They got an eel out there."

Red embers in the fire smouldered in the shallow earthy pit. It was time to put the eel into the frying pan. My friend stirred a lump of stale butter around the pan. Chunky portions of the slimy grey-bellied eel sizzled in a gravy of Fernleaf butter, spitting as the pungent smell of rubbery flesh wafted up our noses. I felt sick to the stomach but I was keen to try this eel. Only later would I discover that the East Tamaki is polluted water.

Aunty Rona opened the front door. Her face was like thunder. "Tau!" she shouted from the bottom step. "You'd better get your arse in here before I bang your ears." She looked at me and shook her head. "Nannygoat? What the hell are you doing? Go on . . . home!"

"But, Aunty Rona," I protested, "we . . ."

"Get your arse home — *now!*"

"Aw . . ."

"Nannygoat, you do as you're told!" She was still shaking her head.

"Yes, Aunty."

I did as I was told, whispered goodbye to Tau and walked away, hearing his mother complain, "Boooyy! You'd better dig in that hole and get your arse in here. You hear me? And you got school in the morning."

Opening my front gate, I could still hear Aunty Rona lecturing Tau, "You been down that river again. Boy, I'm gunna slap your ears. You look at the dirt on your feet. You get inside and, boy, you wash your feet! Hear me?"

f o u r

A DREAM: *I'M* outside the house of my childhood. I'm wandering through the front yard and look up into the sunny blue sky. Before my eyes long grey clouds fester about the sun. The wind comes up, at first a breeze, then, gathering momentum, it begins to howl through the eucalyptus trees. Faster and fiercer the velocity builds until my blond hair is blown into my face. Now the black clouds have blotted out the sun. Away in the distance I see a rotating funnel which grows larger and spins more violently at a rapidly increasing speed. Dirt from the parched summer earth is sucked up into what I now understand to be a tornado. I try to escape, but I don't know where to hide. I daren't seek refuge in the house for I know the approaching tornado will shatter all the windows. Where can I run to?

As I scurry about the front yard the tornado descends upon me. My body is sucked upward into the funnel. I am thrown around in spiralling circles and have difficulty breathing. I fear suffocation and as I'm savagely spun I realise that this storm is of my own creation. Within several seconds, I am spat out. My body is tossed high into the air and I hurtle to the ground at a phenomenal rate. My head and limbs make contact with the ground. For some miraculous reason I suffer no broken bones, no death — I have passed through disaster, remained alive; but am I intact?

I look up to the sky again. The eye of the tornado ceases contact with the earth, and the ferocious twister spirals upward. Losing power, it disintegrates into wispy clouds of grey. Gradually the clouds disperse and a hint of blue breaks through to finally become a clear sky again — and the sun shines.

I stand up from where I have fallen and dust myself off. Brown dirt clings to my clothing and my mouth is full of dust. I'm desperately thirsty and somewhat shaken. I look about me and shudder to see the carnage such a violent freak of nature has left behind. Powerlines are down. Entire sheets of roofing iron are strewn about the street. Cars are upturned and wooden fences have been reduced to splinters. Even more strange is that the roads and houses are deserted. I have experienced such hell alone. More importantly, I have survived.

— There's a storm coming.

— How do you know this, Fourteen?

— I know. Something awful is coming.

— Is it the past, Fourteen?

THE LATE MORNING sun shines through the open window. What day is it? I ask myself.

The voice of Fourteen replies, — Saturday.

I feel anger. God, I can't even keep my thoughts to myself any more!

— Will you go away, Fourteen? Will you just leave me alone?

Her soft, adolescent voice cries inside my head.

— You don't like me. Nobody likes me. I'm trying to help you. We have to survive but you won't accept our presence. She whimpers softly, and before I can resist her need to surface, she has taken the handkerchief from under my pillow and is wiping her eyes.

— My eyes too? Shit, do we share the same eyes?

She stops sniffling. I feel sad and her mouth spreads into a wide smile over my face. We share the same mouth but mine is smaller, she giggles and adds, You smoke too much! and goes on to answer questions I'm thinking.

— My God! You can read my thoughts?

— I can. And you're able to read mine, she beams.

I'm astonished . . . but she's confirmed what I've been thinking for a while. — How?

— I don't know. We're all connected but each of us is different from you.

She seems nervous now. I sense that she is about to fade.

— Fourteen?

— Yes? she cries sadly. I feel her little face melt away from mine.

— So my body is shared?

— Yes, she whispers.

I sense her dread as she slips into the darkness within. She's like a little bird, delicate, small; a sad flighty sparrow living in fear, who skips from one place to another.

I realise that she will be gone in a moment so I quickly call to her within myself, hoping for an answer. — Fourteen. Read my thoughts. I like you.

I hear her crying, but she seems to be shouting at something else within my head, — You can't stop me talking!

My mind strains to listen to Fourteen's voice. It's as though she were full flesh a moment ago and now she's begun to vanish, a ghost leaving small traces of her tears behind. Where does she go? Now I feel ice-cold, fire, hatred, lava. Something is about to boil over. I'm going to get burnt. It's him, Son of Sorrows.

— Where the fuck do you think she's gone?

— You tell me.

— Well, where do *you* go? he snorts.

"Shit," I gasp to discover a blister on the back of my hand. A lighted cigarette has been broken in half and the hot embers have seared into my flesh.

Son of Sorrows is laughing. — You shouldn't smoke in bed! Mind you don't set the house on fire!

I start to cry. — Why are you tormenting me?

— Because I hate you, Nankavelle.

— Why? How can you be so bitter? I'm overwhelmed with a feeling of impending doom. I realise that I haven't been the one smoking. So who lit the cigarette? How could I have possibly been smoking when I've been talking to Fourteen?

— You idiot, curses Son of Sorrows. He breaks into loud, maddening laughter. Does the word SOLDIER mean anything to you? Lion Beer? Do you drink that shit? Ha! So you don't know about Russell yet? Well, well, well! You'll find out sooner or later. The riddle of all of us is yours to solve.

Tears are streaming down my face. My head is a drum being pounded.

— It was *you*, Son of Sorrows, you burnt me!

— Mmm, so I did. I used Russell's smoke. He's been listening in to your conversation with the little bitch . . .

— Why can't you leave Fourteen alone?

— She's just like Trouble, he hisses, a poisonous snake inside me, someone I'm beginning to hate. I'm walking a tightrope, fear beside me and hatred bubbling below, no safety net.

— Trouble? I enquire, having taken the bait.

— You have a lot to learn. He sniggers like a hyena. Still, you could always book into a nice cosy mental hospital.

HE HAS GONE. I know this because my mind is as clear and silent as a polished mirror: no dust, only the clean sweet scent of peace flowing through my head. For now I'm as alone as I should be.

My hand burns. I get up from the bed and walk into the kitchen where I run cold water over the blister. While standing at the sink I think of the things Son of Sorrows has said. Who's Russell? And why would he listen in on my conversation with Fourteen? Who am I? A telephone exchange . . .? I laugh out loud, savouring this inside joke. Good morning, operator. Could you connect me with a girl — um — somewhere in the world. Her name is Fourteen. Tears again roll down my cheeks. I'm crying over the ridiculous notion that there are people inside me. I'm also afraid. I left a soldier in a taxi but . . . what happened before that? And who is Trouble?

I weep uncontrollably. If there were a church nearby I would walk in, kneel before the sanctuary and exclaim, "God? Help me. I think I'm possessed by other spirits." And what would God say? "Come back tomorrow. I'm busy with restless souls at present."

What about my soul? Even God can't help me!

THE BODY SPEAKS:
Happiness is the stomach being awarded a rare and nourishing breakfast. The mouth smiles and the eyes are deep blue. All the strong selves emerge today. Fourteen peers momentarily through the eyes and exclaims, "The sun is out!" because she has forgotten what sunlight feels like. Nankavelle is overawed too. He leans against the open door and enjoys the head-to-foot glow of sunshine sending warm, tranquil thoughts streamimg through him. He too has seen very little of the sun and searches his mind for the reason why. "What season is it?" he asks himself.

A *FAVOURITE PASTIME* of mine when bunking school in the winter was to slip into my father's oilskin coat and don a pair of cotton sandshoes. This was the best season to walk around the rocky shores of the river. The rain would fall heavily and though I was protected from the droplets of water, my teeth chattered and my skin felt as cold and thick as rubber.

I'd stand on the scoured concrete boat ramp with a torrent of water pouring down my chin and the rain slicking my long hair back. A constant drip-drop of rain trailed down my neck. I was utterly happy because it excited me greatly to linger at the river's edge and look across the water.

A thick grey mist loomed over the choppy expanse of muddy brown river, and was wind-blown into my face. Land on the other side couldn't be seen — even the trees, the pylons with a row of moored boats were out of view. I'd open my mouth as wide as I could and inhale that dewy mist, rain spattering onto my teeth. I'd roll my tongue over my lips, tasting the rain with the passion of a writer — memorising a scene for a future novel.

Birds could be heard chirping as they flew overhead but I could not see them until they were right above me. I'd gaze at the violent black sky, wishing I was courageous enough to swim in the river. My eyes hurt and my cheeks stung — such cold rain on my face seemed to intoxicate me. I longed to walk into that forbidding, angry water, become part of the awesome elements of nature.

The blue sandshoes I wore squelched around my frozen toes. My ankles hurt and the cotton tightened against my heel.

To see that water was like looking at a typical scene, preserved in celluloid, from a New Zealand movie: a fierce tidal drag, sand, trees, screeching birds — powerful, intimate, with the added stigma of loneliness, a vague coastal atmosphere. No matter how cold I felt, surely this was paradise. Who'd ever imagine that I was just an eleven-year-old Kiwi kid several hundred metres behind a bland, curving stretch of suburbia?

In the river circles broke, radiated out and into other circles and more circles still. This was like looking at a huge, ugly, crocheted blanket. It had been transformed into a living, vibrant art form by the wind. Every now and then a stream of air bubbles travelled up from between the rocks and blurped on the water's surface. I'd watch this curiously and determine in my mind what type of fish species was advertising its presence to the world.

I felt at peace among all this chaos, this grey day in the eyes of suburbia which probably resented being unable to peg its routine of daily washing on the line. The possibility of impending floods, even the nuisance of sewerage washing into the gutter, was everything a kid like me would call bliss. If I could have taken this utterly wonderful yet supposedly "miserable" day home in my back pocket, I would have! This was the kind of weather I'd have happily played in, forever.

Was I an unusual or crazy child to like the unlikeable? Maybe, back then, when loving the river and the rain, I was filling a time capsule to crack open at a later date — when my instincts would say, Write what you know.

f i v e

THE GAME WE neighbourhood kids play is a battle of speed and
endurance involving rugby tackles. The older kids, the cigarette
smokers, truants and a mummy's-boy all compete in the heart-racing rush.
It is exactly that: a rush. From one side of old Mr Balkam's run-down
property to the other, amongst waist-high weeds. The object of the game
is to tackle the contestants as they charge through the paspalum and fen-
nel. Once tackled, the 'victim' has to tackle the others. Many accidents
occur. A thousand tears and tantrums are hold-ups to the game when big
brothers from neighbourhood families dispense hankies, mop up tears,
cuddle the wounded ones, boot their arses lightly and curse, "Well go on
home, you fuckin' cry baby!"

Those of us kids who are endurers (nevertheless battle-scarred) charge
again across the long weedy yard, our hearts hammering with anxiety and
fear, our eyes scanning around us, proud minds thinking, I'm tough —
they won't catch me. Our legs are scratched and itchy from raw contact
with stinging nettle; blood surges through our nimble bodies. Yet what is
more terrifying is to fail at this game, to be deemed weak, cowardly. Knee
abrasions equal power and status: Look-I'm-badly-injured-but-I'll-keep-
playing. How noble, how utterly fantastic when the mummy's-boy is stung
by a bee — the corner of his eye swollen; the hospital, an injection; aller-
gic to stings; very ill: *Is the hero awake? Is he over the major trauma? Can I
see him . . . adore him? Can the others here, too, worship such a brave and
afflicted friend? Of course — here, take all our lollies.*

We kids sit around the street on hot summer evenings, eagerly skiting
about how we can handle bee stings and exhibiting our scars. Out come
the elbows where fractures happened, etc, etc. All of us neighbourhood
kids are tough, eh!

There's something exciting about the danger involved in playing this
game. A pure adrenalin high. And to survive a confrontation with old Mr

Balkam is to earn the respect of older siblings and to be allowed a "drag" on big sister's cigarette.

"Shit! Mr Balkam's coming. Quick, hide."

"Get down, you idiot! Keep your fuckin' head down, Nankavelle."

"Shut up, Simon — we'll get caught!"

"Nankavelle? What are you laughing at?"

All I can think about is how nervous I am, which is why I'm laughing. The bitter old drunkard, flying along the gravel drive in a beat-up Vauxhall, fills me with dread and loathing. He's an aggressive man and hates to see a swarm of Maori and Pakeha children on the rusting yellow bulldozer in his yard.

Mr Balkam clambers from his car and marches toward us, bellowing with rage. "You little bastards! Fuck off or I'll call the bloody coppers on ya!"

All of us remain dead still but the old Russian knows we're hiding somewhere in the jungle of tall weeds. We cover our mouths to stop the laughter getting out. That poor, drunken, desperate old fool — my God, we push him well over the limit. Next minute he strides over to where we think we're successfully concealed. His feet whistle through the grass, drawing closer, and he's cursing again, "Bugger off, the lot of ya!"

My mind bulges under the strain of a stereotypical image of him, the old Russian, for I've heard the older kids tell stories about him. Is he *really* Russian? Or does that darkly concocted rumour only serve to add to Mr Balkam's fearsome mana, icing our already cold blood as it slides through our veins?

The old man is almost upon us. We leap out of the grass and tear along the driveway like swallows in flight. Our hearts are pulsing and our eyes are itching with hayfever. We cross the road to Tau's house while the older siblings scatter in all directions. Aunty Rona orders us inside and we are lectured severely about going on old Balkam's property. Several minutes later a police car cruises into the street. We watch from Aunty Rona's window, our eyes widening.

"Ooh, Mummy," says Tau's sister, Hine, "the police are here."

Aunty Rona greets two officers at the front door. They come inside and we three are lectured once more about trespassing. The constables shake their heads as if to say, What do you do with these troublesome kids. Aunty Rona closes the front door and orders us into her room where Tau's ears are slapped and I am sent straight to bed.

Another day passes and the kids of No-Exit Street are back on the old Russian's property again, only this time it's to smoke stolen cigarettes and drink wine taken from a neighbour's booze cabinet. And before long that electrifying game of rush and tackle begins all over again.

This time the mummy's-boy from next door is allowed to join in. It is with cruel delight that I tackle the bee-stung hero who is not one any more. He howls like a baby and I'm gloating, satisfied that I'm not the only cry-baby in the neighbourhood.

My brother is doing a lot of tackling and he is merciless. I'm soon bawling my eyes out too because I've a thundering headache, and I'm winded, after being thrown to the ground in a tackle so forceful that I feel I've come out of a road accident (never mind, Chantelle will fuss over me and pull me close to her Raquel Welch tits). Mummy's-boy has had his little sook session and now it's his turn to laugh at me.

On and on, this heaven-and-hell of a game continues — right through the summer nights. I still can't understand the terror I feel when sprinting for the other side. I fear something more than simply being tackled. The anxiety is in the capturing of my body. The bliss is just being a healthy active kid playing games with his childhood companions.

ALONE IN THE house of my childhood. A long red carpeted hallway. The sun streams through the rippled yellow glass on the locked front door. I stand at the end of the hall gazing upon a two-metre-long bookcase, crammed full of books about witchcraft, serial killer mysteries, sexology, psychology, *Reader's Digest*, school encyclopaedias — no New Zealand literature!

I open the kitchen door. My cold feet make contact with the linoleum floor. I'm standing by the fridge, staring at a red Formica table, the one with the rusting steel legs. On the table lies an open horse-racing guide, a packet of Pall Mall plain, no filters. I cough while smoking one of these. I can have anything: money, beer, lollies, potato chips . . . rum and Coke at the adult parties.

— The price you paid . . .

— Get out of here, Son of Sorrows! This is my dream.

— You idiot. Only a fool remembers.

Now I'm walking back down the hallway toward the bathroom. I open the door and again my bare feet touch the linoleum. A chunky, multi-coloured stone pattern jumps up from the floor and makes my eyes burn.

— Reality hurts, you idiot. Get out of this dream now!

— But why, Son of Sorrows? It's only a *dream*.

— Bullshit, Nankavelle. You are walking into a time bomb.

I'm in the lounge now, which reeks of stale beer. My father has pasted up the new wallpaper, blue and gold swirls with deep veins of black and orange: monarch butterfly wings.

Sprawling on the vinyl couch, I light another of my father's cigarettes which I've stolen from the pack on the kitchen table. As I puff and exhale smoke I hear the sound of a car pull up the drive. I run along the hall and enter the bathroom. Peering through the frosted window I see the shadow of a black car outside. I may as well be dead now. I'm in serious trouble.

The big old black beetle is a police car. My heart hammers. Fear itself is knocking on the inside of my chest. My eyes are streaming. They're here to take me away.

Are you going to behave?

Yes! Yes!

There's a policeman on the telephone. He wants to talk to you.

Hello?" My voice is timid, obedient. *Yes, yes . . . I'll be good. Yes, I promise.*

I climb down from the open window and scurry along the hallway, silent on my feet. Carefully I unlock the back door and, passing through the porch, I flee into the garden beyond. They won't find me here. Uncertainty, fear, surging through my body like an electric shock. My hands and feet are numb. My brain vibrates. Many voices are shouting within my head, but I ignore them, thinking of my own safety.

I know! God will help me. God's like that. He does save kids . . . He does! Truly, he does.

THE BLACK POLICE car has gone. I can come out from under the house now. Maybe I should wait a while . . .?

Son of Sorrows thunders through my dream, — Yeah! Scare the bastards! Let them think you've run away. But you're not as clever as me, Nankavelle.

— I don't accept this dream. I want to wake up!

— You wanted the truth. Fuck you, Nankavelle. I told you this was a time bomb.

"God," I gasp, sitting up in my bed. The room is dark and my vision is hazy. I squint at the digital clock which reads 2.11 am. My pyjamas are soaking. Beads of sweat trickle down my brow and mucus runs from my nose. The headache begins, a pulsing, skull-crushing pain which makes tears well up in my eyes. The level of pain increases until I am rolling on the bed groaning, both hands clasped over one side and the top of my head.

— Need a doctor . . .?

— Of course I need a bloody doctor, Fourteen!

"HAS HE BEEN under any stress?"

"Oh, for godsakes! Just stick the bloody thing in, will you."

The doctor takes Audrey aside and questions her just outside the doorway to my room. Audrey is saying that I suffer with a lot of headaches. The young doctor tells her that my temperature is high. A cluster migraine, he concludes.

They enter the room again. Audrey waits by the door while the doctor peels the plastic wrap off an injection.

"This will help with the nausea." He jabs the needle into the soft muscle of my upper arm and frowns.

"Ouch! What are you giving me?" I ask while my arm burns as hot as fire.

"Stemetil."

"But that's for nausea. What about the pain?" I complain.

"Your landlady tells me you have a history of epilepsy," he prompts.

I'm thinking, What about this damned pain! Instead I answer, "Yeah, but what relevance is the epilepsy?" Oh great. I'm going to pay thirty-five dollars for nothing. Stemetil? My arse, it'll help.

The doctor sighs. He looks carefully at me and then asks, "Have you had any seizures today?"

I'm angry now. "Can't you give me something for the bloody pain?" I fold my arms across my chest, gritting my teeth so my words cannot get out. Thirty-five dollars for this?

The doctor reaches into his leather bag and retrieves a foil package of tablets. "Sorry, I can only give you these Panadeine for now. Take two, but no less than four hours apart. I suggest you go to your own GP and get these headaches sorted out."

Anger rises within me like a tidal wave and this makes my headache worse. The increased throbbing is like a balloon full of water that's about to pop and flush spasms of pain all through my head. After a moment I let go of my feelings, give in, lie defeated in this ridiculous situation.

"Thanks, doc," I groan, fresh tears sliding down my cheeks.

"Good, good," murmurs the doctor and he pats my shoulder before placing an account for forty-two dollars on the bedside cabinet. Audrey sees him to the front door, and as the doctor crosses the threshold I hear him say, "Headaches like that need seeing to."

s i x

THE BODY SPEAKS:
Laughter is sporadic. The rib cage expands as, simultaneously, the head is thrown back. Through charming teeth the sound of delight erupts. A woman rolls her eyes, smiles with intended flirtation. Her breasts are pushed forward, the body posture saying, Darling, such humour!

But Nankavelle kills the moment: he's surfaced from that deep inner place and is asking, — What's so funny?

1976. FAMILY AND friends were gathered together on Guy Fawkes night, to eat, to drink and celebrate — or was it just a good excuse to fire up the barbecue, get pissed and have a great time?

And a great time it was for everybody present, in the large backyard of a suburban street in Mt Wellington. My mother's family arrived early in the evening. Grandad was downing a glass of Lion Red, tapping his tartan slippers to the thrum of a banjo which he plucked at with huge ancient fingers. Nana darted in and out of the kitchen, fetching plates, kissing grandchildren as she went past. She reeked of an old lavender perfume, her silvery hair modestly styled and her loving eyes aflame.

"Hello, darling. You're doing well at school, dear?"

I told her I was and this meant that I was happy for a change — and why not? I'd won a Special Terrific Person award at school and had to be brave, taking the red certificate from a mean old headmaster, shaking his hand and whispering, "Thank you."

My mother sat on a kitchen chair which had been placed against the shed. She was talking to her sister, my Aunty Judy. Both Mum and Judy sipped cask wine from short-stemmed glasses. They laughed every now and then, and Mum poured a drink for my grandmother. Mum's hair was long, shiny, auburn. She wore a "boob tube" and dress jeans. She was so elegant, a bundle of nervous energy — who'd ever have thought that her marriage to Dad was on the rocks. Nevertheless, my brother, two sisters and I were very happy that evening.

Cousin Emma stood close to me. We were inseparable, like brother and sister. We laughed and sang along to the rhythm of Grandad's toe-tapping rendition of "She'll Be Coming Round the Mountain".

Dad was chef that night. He looked the perfect picture, a young handsome man, smiling with spatula in hand, turning generous portions of steak over on the smoky grill. His glass of rum and Coke was ever full. He was utterly happy. His brothers and sister smoked and drank and laughed.

I'm not tired. Ugh, bedtime at . . . "Mum? Can I stay up late tonight?"

"We'll see," my father said, standing back from the barbecue and coughing into one hand. He often answered in place of Mum.

"Mummmm!" I didn't want to go to bed.

"Yes, love?" She stretched out one hand and I immediately ran to her, accepting her invitation for a cuddle. I nagged, and Mum deflated my request with the words, "We'll see."

Aunty Judy had a rattling sound coming from her throat and chest. She took a whiff of Ventolin and had another plastic inhaler in her banana-bag for Emma's asthma. Cousin Emma tapped me on the shoulder: "Last one to the apple tree is a pig-snout!"

I let go of my mother's arm and made a mad dash for the tree. Emma was almost there. We collapsed on the summer-warm grass at the base of the tree and laughed. The sky was beginning to darken and mosquitoes whined and whizzed past our ears. And then I had a great idea: "Let's play Three-Legs Men!" Promptly I tied my left leg to Emma's right leg. Giggling hysterically, we cousins hobbled about the yard singing:

> My mummy she told me to open the door,
> But I didn't want to.
> I opened the door and he fell through the floor,
> That crazy man from China.
>
> My mummy she told me to open the . . .

Our skinny eight-year-old legs were tingling at the feel of fat dandelion heads brushing around our ankles. The object of this game was for our two bodies to walk in unison as a three-legged man. What made it more exciting was to gather speed until our free legs couldn't keep up with our common middle "leg", thus we tripped on something, falling into the lush green grass and laughing until we nearly wet our pants.

Back at the barbecue table all the kids, along with Emma and me, squeezed tomato sauce into the crevice of a split sausage, wrapping a thick wedge of buttered bread around it. Our hyperactive little minds soaked up what was going on around us. We laughed at jokes without knowing what we were giggling about, taking our cue from when the adults laughed. We told childish jokes of our own. Just as we didn't understand their jokes, the adults were baffled by what amused us. Our favourite joke came from a television commercial for a soap which a mother lathered into a fat baby's chest. The lyrics went, "Pamper it with Palmolive . . . Your big toes, your tum-tum." Our version had a childlike preoccupation with other body parts: Emma and I chanted ". . . Your big toes, your bum-bum." My cousin laughed so vigorously that she had an asthma attack. We also tittered over words like "poos" and "tits".

Dad's sister and her husband were a young married couple. They flicked through a stack of LP records: Neil Diamond, Carly Simon, Elton John's *Yellow Brick Road* and other titles. This was where the party livened up. Dad's face was flushed, Mum and Aunty Judy were laughing at private jokes and discussing marriage problems.

Grandad and Nana had packed away the banjo and left the party. My two sisters squabbled every now and then until Dad intervened and then they made up before retreating indoors to play with their dolls. My brother talked with Aunty Tina, a glass of beer in hand — Dad's boy — while Emma and I mulled about the barbecue table picking at cuts of warm steak. We'd eaten too much and I was doing the rounds for cuddles. I was an affectionate child and fantasised that I was an adult: I can smoke too!

— No you can't! said an internal voice, another boy-self whom I was familiar with.

Now it was dark and the wind had come up. My father lit the bonfire, a huge mound of wood, branches and a guy made out of paper rubbish bags. The effigy burnt brilliantly and my sisters were standing at the back door waiting for the inferno to die down.

Dad's speech was slurred. Mum walked slowly with an unsteady gait, radiant in her happy housewife mode. At last Uncle Jerome lit the first firework. Our backyard was glowing with a green fog, the smell of sulphur creating an eerie atmosphere. And for what seemed like hours we kids marvelled over hot sprays of molten colours, bursts of red rain, and a volcanic spiral of orange fire as the Catherine wheels spun on the fence.

I began yawning and swaying on my feet. Cousin Emma had sat down beside her mother who comforted her as she wheezed from all the excite-ment. The guests kissed and waved goodbye one by one, keys jangling. The sound of their cars travelling up Panama Road became distant. The party was over. The house was locked, the lights were out, and I could hear my father's snoring through the wall. Another happy moment had gone — but not forever.

I, TH' FUCKWIT, *fink brainy people are jus' a lotta wankers. Vey fink I'm so fick, dat dere's nuffin' 'tween my ears. I don' much like uvver people anyway, 'cause vey talk to me like I's a baby or sumfink. I jus' sit inna corner and wotch the uvvers smilin' and havin' fun. Vey look at me and larf 'cause I answer their questions inna wrong way.*

Lotsa people say fings wot make me angry. Vey say I's a "pea brain" or "fick as a brick shithouse". I get worried 'cause vey'd bang my ears.

When I's mad I see a room fru bright red eyes — it's like a big sea of red and vere's lotsa bangs inside my head. I jus' sit inna corner 'cause I'm dopey. "A fuckwit," vey say.

I'm jus' eighteen but vo I's fick I cin do wot uvvers can't: I cin close my eyes and go to betta places dan dis room of stink people. I know howta make a sling-shot. I cin even shoota target wiv a gun. I cin. I cin smile wiv a good heart inside and know dat I's doin' th' best I cin do in life. I don' fink people are straight wiv me — I'm cleverer thin vey fink 'cause I cin read th' lies in deir faces.

Call me "fick" vey do but I got betta dan dem. I gotta priceless soul inside me 'n' I believe dat God'll answer me preers. I hate false people. I hate liars. I hate vem who use veir fists 'n' mean words. If I's so fick den how come I cin x-ray souls and see th' good lovin' hearts?

When I git pushed over da edge by mean people I git very sad 'n' I blame God for my pain. "Bugger yuh, God!" I ses, "You make life too hard!". . . 'n' I end up cryn' alone in me room.

I cin be betta thin cruel people. I'va heart ov gold — so th' uvvers inside me say.

FLICK! — AND A blinding flash of light penetrates my foggy mind. I'm jolted out of a subconscious dreamland of steamy office windows: smashed vase upon a stainless steel bench. A brain surgeon-cum-psychoanalyst stands over my sleeping body. My lips are blue and the mind-scientist is about to unpick the stitching from a tweed sportscoat I'm wearing. He's saying, "Gay writers should be abolished. You wear the coat of another man. Bad boy! Personality Disorder Number Four!"

I seem to have left the dream but a part of me remains there through a scramble of abstract sequences.

— This is your dream, Nankavelle, Son of Sorrows is saying.

— Some of us want to help you. We like you . . . The voice of Fourteen.

— Men are all the same . . . all the same . . . all the same, Russell adds.

— I should kill the body . . . This is Son of Sorrows threatening again.

— The body? I ask.

— Our body. Ours! fuck you! . . . That anger again.

Momentarily I awaken. The confusion mounts and I re-enter the dream. I'm perplexed at the realisation that I am somehow two: He-adult and He-child (identified by the Others as "It").

— Mental, just like the brother used to say, Son of Sorrows taunts.

— Leave him alone! . . . Fourteen is being brave.

— As mental as the Mad-Child. Wish all of you were dead! Son of Sorrow's anger is overwhelming to all present in this dream.

This absurdity continues.

There's a window view into the Mad-Child's dream, a ringside seat outside his childish world. I fail to grasp the thread of enlightenment, that my emotions and feelings are shared with this child. My link to the child is in the sensations of physical and psychic pain, seeing, hearing, touching, tasting and living out the surrealistic experiences and thoughts of this self in hell. My reality is to absorb now what the child is surviving. We are separate persons but our minds have fused into one.

The madness gathers in momentum. Fear pulses through our mind. A physical sensation of suffocation. I'm an ugly dying fish gasping for air. Explosions of blue light. Was asleep? Am asleep? The child is asking, Who, light. . .? Aw, eyes hurt!

A gradual ebb–flow of facts and fiction, shocking to the senses, past and present all intermingled. Something gropes its way up to the pillow where I rest. A hand . . .? No, an arm . . . two arms. What am I reaching for?

The Mad-Child manages to string together features of the dream. His thought construction is a jumbled logic, void of any chronological order: A window of vases-smashed-stitching a bright light-psychoanalyst-tweed coat falling out the vase-window in the flowers . . .

I am reaching for my own face and the Mad-Child's too, thinking again, Am I awake or asleep still?

Ugly rebukes from childhood sound out in my head:

Stupid, stupid boy!

God, you're ugly.

I hope you drop dead . . . useless little cunt!

You're not my brother!

What's wrong with you? Are you deaf or something!

Wish you'd never been born!

These insults are an aimed missile. Their target: to bruise the Mad-Child.

Now the mind-scientist concludes this abstract dream: ". . . will never lead a normal life. . . in and out of institutions for the rest of his life . . . queer as a two-bob watch. . . Residual Schizophrenia. . . will need medication for the rest of his life . . . sorry, not much I can do but stabilise his acute episode . . ."

s e v e n

*T*HE *LONG WINTER* of 1987 begins amidst my own fears that there is something profoundly wrong with me. At times I have difficulty moving and, as I attempt to walk the pavement I veer sideways, off to the left. My sense of balance is going. When I speak my words slur and I have a nervous tic on the right side of my face. Audrey urges me to book a consultation with Doctor Weste, but I have other things on my mind, security and love foremost.

On a wet Tuesday afternoon as Audrey and I sit by the fireside I confess that I'm very fond of her, that our friendship is important. Like a bolt out of the blue, I take her hand and look deeply into her eyes. "Live with me, Audrey?" I say, at the same time thinking, What the hell am I saying?

She stubs out a cigarette and, after staring intently at me for a moment, exclaims, "But you are living with me! You're my boarder."

"No. No," I say, feeling a nervous build-up of energy in my stomach, "I mean . . . have an affair with me."

She smiles sweetly. "But you're only eighteen years old. I'm a middle-aged woman! My family would think that I'm cradle snatching."

I persist with a cheeky answer. "Let them think that. If they want a toy-boy then they can find one of their own."

"That's not very funny, Matty. Really, I'm flattered but . . ."

"Aw, come on, why should age be a barrier?"

She pats the side of my cheek and tries to make her reply come out as a joke. "You really feel something for me, don't you?" Her laughter is a flush of anxiety.

"Yes, I do," I state seriously, yet a doubt burns through my mind, the voice of my own insecurity saying, Damn it, Matthew, you're lonely.

"I have to think about it, Matty," she says, squeezing her hand over mine.

THAT SAME WEEK, after Audrey and I begin sleeping in the same bed, I visit my parents. I walk into the kitchen where my mother is watering potplants which are on top of the refrigerator. "Hi, Mum."

She turns around to face me and I notice there is a crease running through her brow. She looks worried. "Do you want a drink? I can put the kettle on."

"What's wrong, Mum?"

After pouring powdered milk into two cups she pulls up a chair and offers me a cheese scone. "Adrian and I are moving back to Auckland," she sighs, sadness in her eyes.

She doesn't want to leave — I *know* it.

"Oh," I whisper, feeling a wave of depression sweep through me. "When are you going?" I'm feeling awful because the disappointment must clearly show on my face. I don't want Mum to see that I'm perturbed by the prospect of her and my step-father leaving Christchurch.

"In about two weeks' time. Adrian's getting restless again. He feels there's a better chance of his business succeeding if it was based in Auckland."

"Oh!" is all I can say, and already the anxiety is bubbling up from the pit of my stomach.

"Are you going to keep boarding with Audrey?" She looks even more worried as she asks this and I sense that she views Audrey's as a secure place for me to be.

I spit it out, test her reaction about my living situation. "Mum, Audrey and I are sleeping together."

"Oh, God," she groans, "you mean that you and her are. . ." Her voice breaks into laughter.

I stare at my mother like a wounded soldier. "Muummm!" I growl. "I don't care about the age difference."

"Well," she smiles, her blue eyes glowing, amused at the sheer notion of it all, "as long as you're both happy that's all that matters."

I steer the conversation back to the theme of her return to Auckland. "Where will you both live?"

She says, "With your sister for a while — but let's not talk about that . . . Matt, I've noticed that you haven't been coping for quite some time . . . You're always so distant. Sometimes I look at you and you seem so different. I keep telling Adrian, that's not my son . . . Is there something troubling you?"

My hands shake and I feel as if I could cry. I don't want my mother to leave Christchurch. I feel alone. I'll have nobody but Audrey in my life. The knowledge of my other selves vexes me. Life has begun to turn upside down. I'm caught in a vacuum of silence. Who will understand, let alone believe, that I'm dividing into other selves?

"I'll be fine, Mum." A little white lie.

"You sure?" she asks. "I'm worried about you."

"Really, I'll be fine. I've got to go." I get up from the chair and walk out the back door. I feel sick. Another headache is coming on.

THE BODY SPEAKS:

When the skin fades to a waxen grey and the blood is drained from the face, it signals a severe chest pain. Nankavelle is at the peak of his saddest moments at this time. The aching, crushing sensation of grief. Tears are suppressed because crying in public is not permitted by any of the selves. Shedding of tears is restricted to the sleeping hours of night to guard against nurturing responses from family members. A pillow corner is stuffed into the mouth to stop the sound of grief escaping; the chest is sore from containing it, like an underground explosion building up. Sometimes when the house is empty, the doors bolted, the curtains pulled, every stored-up emotion is let out. After about twenty minutes, the teeth are gritted, the mouth clamped shut, for Nankavelle must "carry on living" as usual. A typical after-effect of releasing pent-up grief is to suffer a cluster migraine.

The body hurts but it is the greatest ally for all selves — it is their fortress. Son of Sorrows despises affections from those outside the Body who are offering physical comfort. Nankavelle too will never allow himself to be the focus of other people's attentions — he shuns the limelight or popularity.

Public life belongs to the Daniels selves . . .

AUDREY CARRIES A large cardboard box through the laundry and drops it on the back porch where I toss kindling into it. I've been chopping firewood for some ten minutes or more. I am about to split more wood when nausea snakes up to my chest from the bottom of my stomach. I feel ill — as in nervous, a fateful sense of doom seizing hold of me. With hands trembling I put down the axe. I freeze in a standing position and gaze at it. All at once I feel dizzy and have an overwhelming desire to run. Run! Run! Where do I run to?

Present time disappears. Coming back into existence is yesterday, long ago. I lean against the house, fearful that I'm going to black out. I seem to be losing control of my body and at the same time I see *him* and the axe. The memory comes. There is nothing but a dream-like quality and the feeling that I'm about to wet my pants . . .

I am almost nine years old, back in that wretched childhood house where I'm perpetually cocooned in a web of fear and dread. My father has been drinking all evening. My sisters are in their bedroom down the hall. My brother and I are in our room trying to sleep. We have been kept awake by our father's shouting and the sound of our mother weeping.

Before bedtime I'd anticipated there'd be trouble later in the evening. I knew this because as I kissed my father goodnight I noticed that his eyes were bloodshot. He was hopelessly drunk and as I pecked his cheek the distinct odour of rum wafted out of his mouth. He'd been making picky remarks about my mother during the early evening, his favourite bitter insult had been to call her a "whore".

There I am lying in bed with my face and body pressed into the wall, which my bed is hard against, when I hear Dad coming down the hall. The bedroom light has been out for three or four hours and now the door is flung open.

"Get up!" he roars.

My brother Peter and I start to emerge from our beds. I cover my eyes because of the harsh light from the hall, and then the sudden switching-on of the bedroom light blinds me with its glare.

"Go into the lounge — now!" My father leaves the room, cursing and swearing, before thundering down the hall to open my sisters' bedroom door. Peter and I stumble down the hallway, weaving left and right on unsteady feet, trying desperately to adjust to the bright light. We can hear our sisters crying and Mum rushing toward my father shouting, "Oh, Gary! Leave them alone!" She is crying and trying to lead my sisters back to bed.

My father explodes with rage again. "Get into the lounge, all of you — *now!*"

Mum argues with him, "You're frightening them, Gary! Leave them alone!" Her voice breaks into sobs. I feel very afraid for my mother. Will he kill her? Will he kill us kids? I know that such dark anger can turn my father into a monster. My dad doesn't love us kids any more — I want to go to bed — I want to go back to bed! My eyes fill with tears, though I know better than to cry out loud.

We four children are seated on the couch, all of us rubbing our eyes. My poor sisters have been woken from sleep. Our father walks around the room, shouting, "Your mother says she's leaving me! Do you want to be without a dad? Would you like to have no mother? I should put all of you in a welfare home where bad kids go, and you'll never see your mother again!" On and on Dad raves. His mouth is twisted up and cruel. From where I sit on the end of the couch I can see tears running down my sisters' faces. Their beautiful blue eyes shed tears of pure fear.

Our mother pleads with Dad to let us go back to bed. Again she shouts, an absolute look of heartache on her loving face, "Gary, the kids! — let them go back to bed!"

Our father loses himself in his anger. He becomes a crying-drunk, irrational, man-monster. He stamps over to the fireside and picks up a small axe. Walking over to the wall directly in front of the couch, in full view of us kids, he places one hand on the wall and splays out his fingers. "Your mother's leaving me! She doesn't love me any more! I have to chop off my fingers! Shall I chop off my hand? Because she doesn't want me any more." He's crying ferociously and so are we.

Dad raises the axe and begins to make chopping motions . . .

I GO WITH Tau and his mother to their relative's farm in Pukekohe.

We board the old green bus which rambles along in lurches and squeals of brakes through the bustling streets of Otahuhu and Papatoetoe. At Hunter's Corner an ambulance with flashing lights and siren blaring jumps the red light and careers off up the road. I think of how lucky I am to be in good health, not to be old with my life trailing into the twilight years. And I'm happy to be on the bus with my beloved Maori friend and Aunty Rona.

Our bus pulls into the kerb outside South Mall, Manurewa, to let an Island family on board. Once we're in motion again Aunty Rona hands us packets of chewing gum from her flax handbag. We spend the rest of the trip with our sticky jaws jabbering and occasionally we tease people boarding the bus until Aunty Rona tells us to behave ourselves or she'll bang our ears. We boys are eager to reach Pukekohe where we will stay for a week with Rona's eldest sister, Aunty Simone.

After what seems like a lifetime of travelling we disembark at Pukekohe and head for the taxi stand. I love the streets of this township, everybody is brown and smiling. The shops are crammed full of lush, big vegetables and signs advertising current specials of taro, potato and onions, which are heaped up in cardboard display boxes.

Aunty Rona hurries us kids along the grassy verge after the taxi driver has been paid. We follow the bare earth tyre tracks around the curving drive, on and up to the house. Now Aunt Simone hurries out from the old weatherboard villa and greets her sister and nephew with a hug and kiss. About her feet circles the family pet, yapping. Rex is a small black and white fox terrier with arthritic legs. He has distinct markings on his torso and legs, like a map on the side of a Friesian cow. I'm also hugged and kissed by Aunty Simone and then we are ushered into the house where a kettle is about to whistle on the stove top.

Aunty Rona unloads bags in another room and returns to the kitchen where she hands her sister a bag of fresh kumara — from Pukekohe, of course! We boys venture into the sitting room and warm our hands by the fire which burns a cosy orange. We start to joke about, pushing and shoving each other for a place on the wide roll-armed sofa. I'm intrigued, after settling on my side of the sofa, to see a hole in the lounge floorboards. Tau and I begin a discussion about the probability of rats coming up through the floor and scurrying about the house. Our words take on a sinister tone as we thrill ourselves with horror stories about fat, sleek rodents on the rampage — the rat version of Alfred Hitchcock's *The Birds*.

Aunty Simone enters the lounge with two huge tin mugs of tea. We spend ages afterwards hurrying to and fro, from lounge to kitchen, stuffing our faces with hot slabs of Maori bread and Marmite. All the while Rona and her sister are talking about the farm and catching up on family news. Every now and then Aunty Rona hollers from the kitchen, "Tau! Nannygoat! I'll slap your ears if you swear — hear me?"

We boys chime an obedient "Yes" in unison, at the same time giving the fingers and muttering obscenities under our breath.

The view from Aunty Simone's lounge window is an enormous field of freshly hewn red earth. Tau reckons that onions will be growing there soon. As we run about the house, playing skids in our socks, we note that in a paddock to the south of the house stand two old horses. We're quick to slam the side door on our way out into the yard. The old horses shift listlessly from hoof to hoof, bearing the full sun, and they stare at us with wary but gentle eyes. They stretch their sweaty necks over the fence as we offer them cobs of old corn which we've pinched from the sack in the garage.

The evening arrives too quickly. Bored and restless, we boys fight over the accusation that one of us is cheating at a game of poker. Both of us are sleeping top and tail on a bed in the lounge. Angrily we kick one another and fight over the blanket. The house grows quiet apart from Aunty Rona coughing once in a while, and the faint glow of her cigarette can be seen in the darkness over by the couch.

Next morning I'm awoken by the sound of Tau greeting his uncle with cheeky banter somewhere at the other end of the house. Half asleep, I stumble from the bed and make my way into the kitchen where Aunty Simone puts a mug of steamy tea in front of me. Uncle Robert greets me with a weary "Hi" — he doesn't much understand why his sister-in-law has brought me to the farm and probably feels resentment towards my parents who abandoned their friendship with him some years earlier. Nevertheless, after a hearty breakfast Uncle Robert takes Tau and me out into the paddock for a game of soccer.

The funniest incident happens: I'm racing towards the ball, preparing to kick it, and as I do I slip on a cowpat. My body slides along the grass and I make head contact with the cowshit — face down. With absolute horror and humiliation I storm off to the house, to the accompaniment of my friend's laughing and jeering, utterly disgusted that I have cowshit not only on my face but also in my mouth. At the back door Aunty Simone greets me with a compassionate smile. She leads me into the bathroom after filling the tub with hot water. I bathe in a mixture of water and shit, a rage building like an inferno within.

The bath fascinates me, for it is so big two grown-ups could fit into it easily. It even has claw feet which remind me of horses' hooves or perhaps — and now imagination slips into overdrive — demon's feet.

After some gentle fussing over me, Aunty Simone helps me get over my mood and perk up. I am to laugh about the cow pat incident some hours later, even when my friend whoops with laughter to recall the event in lurid detail.

What we boys like to do at night is look up at the stars from one end of the bed. We believe that time here at the farm will stretch on forever. It doesn't. Soon we are on the old green bus heading for our stop at Otahuhu.

Returning to No-Exit Street brings more fishing expeditions at the river, the usual secret places to smoke cigarettes we've nabbed and talk about Chantelle's big tits and if she's still (or ever was) screwing Murray aboard his boat.

e i g h t

"DON'T WAIT UP to see us off," she says, "we'll be leaving in the early hours of the morning." A pause. Mum dips her head for a moment. She looks sad. "I'll write to you . . ."

"Oh, Mum," I whisper, sighing, "I'll be fine." I manage to conceal my sadness. I'm acting, just like my mother. When a moment is painful — head up, kiddo, smile to the world. I wrap my arms around her shoulders and cling to her tightly. I want to hold on, to cry. As mother and son we are saying goodbye to a two-year legacy of pain.

I once lived in that cosy little home with Mum when we first moved up from Invercargill, just after my sixteenth birthday. I became gravely ill at the time of moving. Strange science fiction thoughts entered my mind. I stopped going out. I ceased reading and watching television and lay around, seldom sleeping at night. Hallucinations of ugly, mean-eyed demons shouted degrading insults at me. Was I cursed? The situation became so bad that I lost contact with reality. My mind had flown out of my body and become lost in outer space. At times I had giggling bouts or threw tantrums of rage like a small child. I felt that black, putrid demon invade my inner world. He manifested through my body in words and action to say and do horrible things. He was unadulterated hatred. Not until two years later would I learn that his name was Son of Sorrows.

It was like being on a roundabout. I was spinning and reeling, weaving my way along a path of self-dissolution, self-loathing, and this private world was again to be diagnosed as an acute schizophrenic episode.

For a brief time I stayed in Sunnyside Hospital, finding the experience to be totally insulting and demeaning: I was monitored and observed, medicated, locked up in a pink cell with a potty to urinate in, subjected to interviews with doctors and psychologists which seemed to be more like brutal interrogations, and told by nurses that I was "a very sick lad!".

The hospital stay was not to prove curative. It was, in fact, to be relived in later years of private therapy as a traumatic period of intense fear and emotional abuse at the hands of one of the nursing staff. Most of the time I was a stupefied idiot due to regular doses of Chlorpromazine, a drug which induces lethargy, headache, nausea, dry ejaculation and a feeling of perpetual exhaustion. By the time I came out of Sunnyside I was feeling as if I'd been run over by a bus.

I went home to my mother's place with a sense of impending doom weighing over me. My other selves began to surface frequently. I knew some of their names but kept their existence hidden from my GP and family. Any switch of self was explained away by my family as "He's in a schizo mood". My so-called moods changed like each emotion was a ten-second flick in time, but secretly I knew they were a fleeting appearance of yet another self. Sometimes I suffered long bouts of amnesia — for some reason unknown to me, some selves were blocking their existence from me.

Through this apparent "schizophrenic episode" the idea of having Multiple Personalities never occurred to me. I held private conversations with people in my mind and they were adamant that they were distinctly separate from myself. I loved and hated them. They were my friends, my enemies — my demons! Their voices talking in my head were what hospital doctors mistakenly identified as thought disorders typical of acute schizophrenia. The so-called hallucinations were a visual extension of all my internal anxieties, rages and fears, which simply became too overwhelming to remain contained within my head. Thus whatever I feared was projected from my mind and appeared before me — a manifestation of fragmented childhood memories.

For two years I underwent a slow and painful recovery from what I can only describe as an intense overload of unresolved childhood conflicts, or if you like, breakdown. And suddenly, like awakening from a nightmare, I found myself at age eighteen having an affair with my landlady Audrey, and saying goodbye to my mother.

I HAVEN'T SLEPT tonight. I feel grief regurgitating when I hear Adrian's motorbike roar to life in the early hours of the morning. They are leaving for Auckland. I have Audrey asleep beside me. I have my wonderful friendship with Ugly-Bug. I have nine different bottles of drugs in the kitchen cupboard — but what do I have?

HOW COULD I have possibly contained such excitement? I was eight years old. The house was still dark in the early hours of the morning. Mum and Dad were in bed. My two sisters, brother and I were crouching around the Christmas tree and passing between ourselves neatly wrapped gifts.

I tore open the bright red and blue wrapping paper. The box in my hands was oblong, similar to the cardboard and plastic trappings which entombed the Barbie doll that greatly pleased my sister Cassandra. Surely Mum and Dad hadn't gift-wrapped a doll for me? If so, it'd have to be male: a role model, a friend . . . a fantasy.

Secretly I loved him from the moment he fell out of the cardboard casing into my eager hands. An Action Man doll — black boots, army camouflage tunic and trousers. His black hair was a short-back-and-sides cut, his eyes gorgeous blue and his mouth as beautiful as his finely sculptured face. Our love affair began. Yeah, he was plastic, but I'd bring him to life in my far-from-innocent imagination. I didn't want to be an eight-year-old boy back then. I had a sudden urge to grow up, to be an adult. I wanted Action Man to be real. Wish became desire, desire became obsession: I want a man like him when I grow up. I want to kiss a real, live Action Man. After carefully peeling away the army attire, disappointment hit home: Where's the diddle?

My little hero enjoyed his swims in the bathroom basin. He was muscular with little inverted nipples and never complained of the cold. He didn't protest when I held him to my chest — kiss, kiss, kiss. Mum said men don't get married to other men when they grow up. Why not? I felt disappointment again, but then determination: I am going to marry a man when I'm bigger — yes, I am!

Fantasy soon turned to boredom. I didn't need Action Man any more — Huh, plastic! — and before long I became frustrated, realising not all dreams could come true. I bent his legs out of shape, lost his black boots and eventually his clothes. If I couldn't have real skin, I wasn't prepared to accept second best — Plastic! You dumb Action Man! No more kisses, no swims! My hopes thwarted, I abandoned him, probably breaking his plastic heart. He might cry now?

I never looked back.

I HAVE BEEN aware of Terry's presence for over a year now. I first discovered the Englishman's existence at the age of sixteen. I was walking along the banks of the Avon River feeling deeply self-conscious, in fear of the world. I'd hyperventilate whenever I ventured outside my home in Dunn Street. It was the equivalent of an execution: I'm going to die in a minute, I can't breathe . . . Why am I so scared? Pure fear. And, like an ambulance at the edge of the cliff, Terry was there.

— Nankavelle, he said, whatever are you afraid of?

— Everything. My light-headedness was overwhelming. I didn't ask his name but realised he spoke with a warm English accent.

— I've been carting you around this river for weeks now. Sure, I can hear your thoughts . . .

— What do you mean? I felt like diving into the river and drowning myself.

— You often arrive home, wondering if your strolls around here did happen . . .

— So? I felt idiotic. My god, I was talking to a voice inside my head again!

— You know, when you can't handle it, I carry the body around here . . .

— So? The clear water looked enticing.

— You may call me Terry . . .

I'M IN A deep hot bath. I don't like hot baths. Beside me on the enamel ledge is a facecloth. My face stings. As I step out of the bath and reach below the mirror for a towel, a vague command flitters through my mind:

· — Look up, he is saying. I'm real.

— You again? Did you run the bath? I didn't run it, for godsakes!

The name "Terry" is finger-painted on the steamy mirror in large capital letters which are melting into streaks of condensation.

— I'm sick of this. . . I'm really angry! What is this? A game of hide 'n' seek?

— Be a detective . . .

— Why? I'm unsure whether I'm questioning "him" or myself. Can I erase time?

— We all do.

— Go away! I feel sick to my stomach. Raising a wet hand to the mirror, I wipe away his name.

— It's Terry. I won't let you forget my name now you know I exist . . .

— But you're not real. I thought you were . . .

— A hallucination? goads Son of Sorrows.

With all my powers of concentration I try to will Son of Sorrows out of my mind. He is a sick and ugly genie who, somehow, has been let loose inside me, and I can slam him back under his jack-in-the-box lid . . . can't I?

I open the bathroom door. My towel?

— In the bath, Nankavelle!

Sure enough, as snidely suggested, the towel is in the bath. It has sunk to the bottom and is sucked toward the plughole which makes gurgling noises before clogging up.

A warmth fills me. Her giggle reverberates through my head.

— Fourteen?

— Yes?

— How long have you known about Terry?

— Who? She sounds puzzled.

— No games, please, Fourteen.

— Another of us? She's hesitant.

THERE'S A BLACK swirling vortex and I'm descending into it. Going . . . going . . . blank, nothing. The real world has gone, as quickly as a slap in the face. I ponder the concept of time. What *is* time?

— You don't need it.

— Oh yes I do! Terry? Is that you? What am I doing here?

— We're at the TAB. Relax . . . only a dollar each way.

"Sir? Sir! Can I help you?" a cashier is asking.

I feel myself receding again, blacking out, entering a deeper level.

"Sorry. I was a bit preoccupied. One each way, thank you . . ." and Terry takes hold of the ticket, smiles, and turns his back on the cashier.

Shards of consciousness — waking, sleeping — awake, asleep — Stanmore Road! At least I recognise this place. But where am I going?

— You're not. I'm heading home. The race is at two.

Such self-assurance, but do I like this man? Another blank. There's a screwed-up ticket on the couch beside me, a can of beer in my hand. He lost the race — serves him right! Now I am in conflict like the other selves, fighting one another, their desperate hands grasping at the slippery net of time. Waste of money — who wants to follow the horses, anyway? Now I'm swigging from his can. Yuck! Lager.

I'M SOON TO accept that Terry has a special function: he steps into my body, allowing me to have a public life — otherwise I'd never stir outside my front door. I'm also surprised, after a glimpse of him in the bathroom mirror, that Terry is in his mid twenties. Impossible, I'm not even twenty yet! But Terry was there alright. I saw him briefly. His eyes were green, his face thin and he was smiling.

— I can help you, okay? he said.

I shrank back from the mirror, angrily telling myself, You're mentally ill. He *can't* be reflected there!

— Don't deny my existence, pal. Strike a light, you know there are others . . .

— But I'm crazy!

— I'm *real* alright, he emphasised. — I can help you.

What choice do I have in all this? I have to be honest. There are "others" within me. I know some of their names, have seen their faces on occasion, and even felt my own face changing form in the process.

Before long I lean on Terry, my PR man, to face the world. Often I am there, behind him, fading out into the security of a black relaxing anaesthesia which erases time whenever I can't cope. My conversations with Terry are very interesting. I grow to love and depend on him after several months of hiding behind him while he surfaces to "carry" The Body around the riverside.

He teaches me many things. His passion is gardening and he is an avid bird-watcher, calling thrush and myna birds by name. I'm safe in my warm dark cocoon while Terry identifies plant life in the gardens of houses facing the river.

— Terry, I'd say, why do you talk to the pensioners around here?

— They're lonely. You'd be able to relate to that, no problem . . . and he breaks up a slice of dry bread and tosses it into the Avon for the ducks.

Terry begins to dress The Body in his own style of clothing: woollen vest, tweed cap, and brown leather shoes are among his trademarks. I often open the wardrobe and ask myself, Where did that woollen scarf come from?

— Me, pal, he says. I bought it.

I feel at ease, close the wardrobe door and laugh to myself.

SOMETIMES HURTFUL PHRASES come to mind. I cry to remember them:

You're just a fuckin' little animal — what are you?

Leave him alone, the mental little idiot!

The eleven-year-old boy running along the hallway. He is sobbing his heart out, and a sound like an explosion is ripping through his skull. It aches as if it would burst open. He's holding his head in both hands now because the noise, almost volcanic, is devastating. His vision is splitting into a two-way tunnel while strange sounds and other voices are possessing his mouth, mind, and body. Gradually the tunnel closes. Another person now walks calmly along the hall.

— Cody can protect you. Yeah, she'll protect you . . . And she fights other selves to remain surfaced.

The torment within that child's home has become unbearable, but he feels reassured by Cody's internal promise.

n i n e

THE BODY SPEAKS:
Sexual desires begin inside the head, excitement flowing from the brain into the eyes whose pupils dilate. The head is pulled up, shoulders back. The soothing tones of conversation are as charming as a bouquet of blood red roses.

In a flurry of internal orders, the Children retreat into the abyss. Both nipples are hard and tight as dried raisins and a fire begins within the head, chest, and groin. The scrotum aches. The heart rate accelerates. Very shortly the lips will be poised, awaiting a kiss. Eyes and hands prepare for exploration. Then, as suddenly as sex begins, frightened selves destroy the moment: mouth closing, body retreating from embrace, eyes downcast, voice forming the words, "I've got to go." And so desire is extinguished yet again.

NEXT DOOR TO where I lived at the end of No-Exit Street, there was a family of eight children. The Dawsons were a friendly clan and I spent a great part of my childhood with Michael, the middle child amongst seven brothers. He was the black sheep of the family and was always arguing with his older brothers. Once he confessed to me that he suspected he'd been adopted by his parents as a small boy. I believed him, too young to realise that my friend had psychological problems. Today his pain would be diagnosed as "Depression".

Michael had a problem with alcohol and drugs. In his company I soon learnt how to "shotgun" marijuana, which was like kissing: the joint was put ember-end into the mouth and smoke was blown backwards through it and inhaled by the receiver through the mouth or nose.

A tough and lonely adolescent, Michael would often sneak out of the house when his family were asleep. He'd gatecrash local parties, getting so blind drunk or stoned that he wouldn't return home until his parents were at work the next day so he'd avoid their confronting him. He had a brilliant career at school, taking top marks for truancy.

When Michael was fifteen and my parents had left No-Exit Street, leaving us kids to our own devices in the family home, I frequently spent days and nights in his company. I was thirteen years old when I spotted my first tiny dot of hashish with him. Mr and Mrs Dawson had gone to work and I had telephoned Michael early that morning to ask if I could come over the fence to his place for a while. When I entered the house I found Michael hovering about the kitchen by the stove where he had the flat edge of a butter knife lying over a glowing hot element.

"Want some hash?" he beamed. The expression on his face said it all. Christmas had come, fun times, laughter. We were to get high together.

"Is it addictive?" I asked with cowardly reserve.

"Nah." Michael was nonchalant. "It won't spin you out. You'll be fine."

"Okay." I was terrified at the thought of what we were up to in his parents' house. I stood beside him watching the knife intently before he took it off the hot ring.

"You ready?"

"Yeah. What do I do?" I was more of an expert at drinking beer than toking on dope.

My friend laughed. "Fuck, you're green, man! When I drop this hash on the hot knife sniff it up fast. Ready?"

"Yeah," I said, wondering how such a small brown lump of wax-like substance could ever get me high. Michael dropped the hashish onto the knife and I immediately bent my face toward the bench and inhaled deeply, first through my open mouth and then through my nose. The resin-like stench was being drawn up through my cupped hands.

I was instantly transported. Within several seconds I had a severe case of the giggles and, to my horror, the whole world tipped to a forty-five degree angle. "The room's going downhill," I gasped, my head a reeling orb of madness.

"My turn," Michael laughed, reheating the knife. "Fuck, you should see your eyes. You're wasted, man." When it was time for him to drop the hashish on the knife, the brown lump accidentally landed somewhere on the linoleum. For what seemed like hours the two of us searched every inch of the floor. Michael was beginning to despair. "Fuck, I paid a mint for this stuff."

"We'll find it," I reassured him. In actuality I was panicking because my adventure into Wonderland was becoming frightening:

— You idiot, Nankavelle, you realise that somebody is going to get into trouble. Michael will want sex, you know. Thirteen years old and you're already fucking about with adult stuff.

— Can it, Son of Sorrows! He can take care of himself, an unknown voice said.

— You fucking homo! Michael's spreading all sorts of shit around the neighbourhood about you.

Suddenly I was aware that my lips were moving: God, they're talking out loud!

Michael shouted, "Got it!" He stood up from the floor. His face was aglow as he placed the knife back on the red element. After inhaling some hashish he burst into laughter and led me from the kitchen, saying he wanted to go into his room. As I followed him along the hall I began to realise that the unfamiliar voice in my head, the one called Son of Sorrows, had spoken some truth. In the bedroom Michael retrieved a *Penthouse* from under his bed. We looked at all the pictures and, after some length of time, my friend unzipped his jeans. His cock was thick and hard within his hand and he asked me to touch it. Shyly I reached out and handled it. Only then did we lie down on the bed.

Another self surfaces — who I'm later to identify as Russell — and I cower behind him, afraid of sex, unsure why the hashish has caused different people's voices to speak to me inside my head. I have a feeling that I know this other self, a vague familiarity, and that sex with Michael is almost *déjà vu*. With the deft touch of a true professional, a master of eroticism, Russell brings my friend to the brink of orgasm.

"Oh, man, I'm gunna come," Michael groans.

— Gunna what? I aim the question at Russell, the one who is in control: the situation now begins to seem like a replay of recent events from this self. A memory comes to mind: It's late at night. Michael and I are sitting on the back doorstep of a neighbourhood house. He is reaching out to rub the front of my jeans. Oral sex. Did I do that? With *him*!

— Matthew Nankavelle, you have a lot to learn!

Am I a homo like Michael and my brother say?

Michael jumps off the bed at the sound of a car pulling up the drive. He runs to the window and peers through the curtains. "Fuck, it's Steve. He's come home from work. Quick! Help me straighten the blankets."

We pull the bedding together as best we can and sprint down the hall where we lock ourselves in his bedroom. I feel sick with fear.

Why am I doing these things? Why is the voice talking inside my head?

Footsteps pad along the hallway carpet. Steve tries to open the door. "Michael!" he yells. "Open up! I know you've been wagging bloody school!"

t e n

THE PSYCHOLOGIST *I* visit is Ralph. During my first time in his
bright, warm office the Mad-Child makes his presence known. He
giggles and makes body movements which completely contradict what I,
Matthew Nankavelle, am trying to say.

I'd like to spill my guts, latch onto Ralph's shirt collar and shout,
"Help, I'm sinking into an unconscious realm of oblivion!" I'm ashamed
that after my harrowing childhood I have evolved into a tragic and somewhat pathetic youth. The word *homosexual* looms at the forefront of my
mind. Of course, I'm quick to disown such inclinations — Russell's to
blame, he's the queer one. I'm skating around the rim of my life's most
bitter chalice: denial of my sexual orientation.

Ralph is listening carefully to what the Mad-Child is saying — and to
what I'm saying — that is, Who am I? The psychologist keeps his face
expressionless but his eyes tell me what I'm certain is going through his
head: One hell of a messed-up kid has just come into the room!

And I'd like to tell him, "I have no control over time, no control over
what my mouth is saying, no memory of today or yesterday. . . Who brought
me here? What's wrong with me? Am I alive? If I exist, then where? How
can I be here today and suddenly gone in five seconds' time?"

It would be an enormous load off my shoulders if Ralph said something
like, "Take these tablets. You have Disorder Number 47. Sleep well, and
tomorrow you're cured!" Fat chance there is of that happening. Yet I like
this man. His wonderful mind intrigues me. But when he puts on his
spectacles I want to attack him for some unknown reason — he's become
the enemy.

A waterfall of words burble out of me, and the next thing I know is
that Ralph is saying, "I may be able to help you. . ." as I wish him goodbye, close the door behind me, and I'm left to my fear of walking along
the street. Curling up inside myself at the traffic lights, a block from

Ralph's office, a new memory comes to me of Russell filling in a question-naire during the consultation. He also wrote a sexual fantasy about Men-Men-Men and I helped hold the pen, ashamed of my sexuality — I'm not like that! Gradually I remember the varied style of conversations I had with Ralph. What perplexes me is that even what I do recall has bits and pieces missing. The therapist's own replies are fractured, as if I've tuned in and out of his words. Someone inside me is editing time itself — me?

"Childhood? Ralph, I don't know . . ." I cut the sentence short because I am confused, but the psychologist gently nudges me to continue.

"Go on."

I don't know how to answer that. "My childhood? Um. I don't remem-ber. Everything . . ."

"The past?" he enquires.

"Everything is so dim. I recall something and then it's gone."

"Don't pressure yourself. Let any memories come up of their own accord."

"I feel like other people. . ." I'm daring now, taking a big risk. He'll think I'm mad. Me and my big mouth!

"People?"

"Did I say that?" I'm faking surprise. I'll have to lie through my teeth to get out of this one.

— Yes, convince this shrewd and observant man that we don't exist!

— Terry? Oh, go away.

Ralph clears his throat. "You were saying that you felt like other peo-ple . . ."

"Uh?" I still fake surprise. I can't lie, I just can't!

— Fucking wimp! sneers Son of Sorrows.

I try to change the subject. "Felt like other . . ." I pause and focus my mind on a table ornament, a blue china bull. "I like that."

Ralph smiles. "Yes, it was a gift from someone a few years ago."

Phew, got out of that one.

The psychologist is still smiling, his intelligent eyes looking deeply into my face. "You felt like other people . . .?"

Shit! "What do you mean?" I'm a terrible liar.

"Don't play games. You're avoiding me."

"Am I?" Come clean!

"Okay, don't tell me. We can sit here all day if you like." Ralph is showing signs of annoyance.

I feel myself fading.

"All day!"

— Just like the father, eh? Son of Sorrows is rolling his eyes and staring at the psychologist.

"We can terminate this session if you like. You're wasting my time." Ralph means every word that he is saying.

The Mad-Child surfaces. Ralph prompts him to talk but all he's able to do is laugh and readjust his body position every few seconds. He's afraid. He doesn't see Ralph or the office, doesn't hear the traffic pass on the busy road outside. The Mad-Child can only hear the sound of his own face being slapped. His memories are fragmented but his face hurts as a voice from the past demands, "Stand still while I'm talking to you! And that's for back-answering me. Do you understand me?"

"Yeah."

"Do you? Do you!"

"Um."

The Mad-Child is trapped between the reality of his childhood home and the presence of Ralph in a downtown office of Christchurch city.

"Speak to me," prompts the psychologist with a gentle kick of the Mad-Child's foot, but now I've surfaced again.

— He fucking well knows we're here! I try to contain Son of Sorrows behind my nervous face.

Ralph looks at me and his expression is deadpan. "What does it feel like to be other people?"

"Eh?" I'm still evasive.

— Tell the Shrink nothing! commands Son of Sorrows.

Again I change the topic of conversation while feeling guilty for dodging the truth. Ralph is really annoyed now. Fourteen is saying she wants to surface, to greet my psychologist, but I won't allow it.

COOL! I CAN do anything now. Woo, you should see what I can see from here. Faaark, we're gathering speed. Come on! Put ya foot flat to the pedal, driver — come on! What! Aw, mister, don't let that thing overtake us . . . I'll wait till that dork pulls up beside us — show him what a wanker he is. Raise my fist to the window and give him the fingers. Oh, whhaaatt! He's an old man. Come on, grandad! Woo hoo, old man, burn that rubber, you old fart! Aw, dork. Turn the corner when the going gets tough, eh? What are ya, old man? . . . My gum, where is it? Come on, guys, who stole my chewing gum? You, Fourteen?

Nah, she's too woosie for that . . . What a dumb city — why do I have to live here? Catching crappy old buses. One day I'm gunna drive a car, a real fast car with mags —— ah, lovey dovey! She's really got the hots for him. Why him? He's bald! Ugh, old and ugly. No way am I ever gunna get that ancient. Ugh! Ooh, bet they kiss each other. Ooh, and they have . . . Man, I never wanna get that old and wrinkly . . . Hey, why've we stopped? Stupid driver. What's he doing? A baby! She better not bring it on this bus. Ooh, know what she's been doing. Who wants sookie babies anyway? . . .

Get real angry when the others say I'm just a kid. I'm not a kid! May only be twelve but I can look after myself. 'Course. It all sucks, man! I'm not as babyish as they think I am. Bet none of them can win money like I do. I don't need them. I'll do as I like. Hah, stinkers! — call me an Adolescent. Just leave me alone. Do what I like in town.

eleven

DAWN. *I SIT* beside Aaron as he lies asleep. Beyond a canopy of
ancient pine trees, the moody blue sky changes colour. The sun is
coming up, slivers of light breaking around fat shadowy cloud formations
— proof that another day is beginning.

The water is gurgling against rocks below the cluster of trees. A full tide
is in, and in less than six hours the tranquility of this place will be shown
up for what it really is: a large, wide river flowing past sloppy grey mudflats.

My body is thirteen years old but I'm the one who really wants to be
here, beside a friend as he sleeps — heart in my mouth, loving him. How
can a man of my age possibly reveal the sensations that sweep through
this body? (I'm stuck here in your body — damn, you kid, I'm trapped in
your childish body!)

I'm experiencing deep turmoil. Suppose I tell Aaron how I feel? Will I
ever be able to love him fully? I'd like to hold him, kiss him, like to take
off my clothes and say, "Here I am. You want me? Here I am."

This is the cruel hand of fate which has imprisoned me inside a young
male body. If I dare express such grief or pain, I'll drive the child from its
body and somehow magically force the body into adult growth. If I could
express myself sexually . . . if, if! And there next to Aaron's sleeping body
is the large cassette deck playing Foreigner's song, "I Want to Know What
Love Is".

A full sunrise now, light warming the morning air, birds stirring in the
trees — it's all too much! I'm filled with a kaleidoscope of emotions, the
cock is hardening. What use am I in this immature body?

Foreigner continues to pour out of the radio. The music is dramatic.
I'm lovesick. I'm happy and sad, but rendered useless because the boy is
making his presence felt.

— See that beer? I address the child within while looking longingly at
Aaron. — If I can't have *him*, kid, you can't have a sip of beer! After a

lengthy stare across the water, I grab hold of the DB bottle, take a long drink, just to make my point. — Get lost, kid! Tears are forming in my eyes.

Love isn't meant to be about violins and soul-sadness but I have no choice in the matter: love from a distance, stew over what could be — hate the child.

A memory is coming. I'm getting it in drip-feed, hiding behind the child's own presence now, soaking up his recollection. It is a bitter memory for me, a stupid prank seen through the child's own eyes. He rationalises it: being kissed by Aaron one night a week ago when Aaron had been drinking and the child was watching him from across a crowded room. Aaron came over to him, smiling, placing one hand on the back of his head and another on the right side of the jaw. For that brief moment I had staked my claim to the body . . .

Aaron's mouth met mine and the next thing I knew, the child had pulled away and stood shaking his head. Visitors in the lounge erupted into laughter and the boy stood there clutching the beer bottle in his hand. He walked out of the room and went to his bedroom. He felt like a fool, and sat on his bed and cried.

I so badly wanted to reproach the child, to hate him for ruining my moment. I had wanted to return Aaron's kiss with full mouth contact but that situation could have got out of hand — how would the child explain such adult behaviour to those at the party? I'd happily have allowed something more to develop, except that the implications of such an action were too close to the bone for me to ignore. . .

What sort of man would I be if I allowed my presence to become intimately physical? Would I allow a child's body to be used as a vehicle for my own sexual gratification? No thanks, I'd rather continue loving Aaron from afar, without intimate body contact.

The memory fades now. I'm crying silently into my hands beside the man whom I love. I sit for hours — dreaming, what if? The sun is well above the sparkling green waters of the Tamaki River. When Aaron wakes up I'll ask him to take me home — drop me off at the gate.

I'M A TEENAGER now, and desperately want to grow up. I'm shaving the blonde fuzz on my face each morning. Soon the hairs will turn black and I'll grow a beard.

My penis is surrounded by a growth of pubic hair. I can even "spoof".

63 /

I'm becoming an adult. I'll smoke cigarettes and my voice will deepen. I'll get a job, go out and drink with friends. I won't be a kid any more. My parents won't tell me what to do and I'll lead my life and take care of myself. I don't want to be "just a kid". I'm not a child and don't want to be told this and that. Hurry up, God, if you really are up there somewhere — hurry up and make me grow up. I'm so desperate to be older. I'll have some say over my life. I'll be important. I'll be respected. Oh please, heavenly Father, age me because I can't stand being a kid any longer.

It seems God heard my call and wasted no time. The body is thirteen but I'm not.

"Mum," I begin, one night at the kitchen table. "I'm in love. . ."

"That's nice," she says, for her eyes see the child body and fail to recognise the burgeoning adult inside.

"Mum."

"Yes, love?"

A burst of confidence. I'm as serious as a biblical pronouncement. I'm strong. I'm breaking free. I'm adult.

— Don't say it, a wimpy boy inside is begging. I push him to one side like a doll you throw across the room because you're bigger than it. You hate its plastic eyes, and you're stronger because you're real — you exist! I speak an urgent truth. "Mum, I'm gay and I'm in love with a man."

"What?" The expression on her face is bewilderment but I can read her mind through the blank vexated stare of her blue eyes. She's thinking, Gay? I knew that all along. And the anxiety which precedes a long minute's silence has me knowing that my mother's heart is saying, My God, my son is gay. Where did I go wrong? What do I say?

I interrupt her cocoon of silence. "Mum. . ."

Her face straightens. "You're only thirteen. These feelings will pass."

"I love him, Mum."

A lengthy conversation follows. I have nothing to hide, nothing to fear. I'm an adult in this child body. A heavy dose of reassurance is needed, so I tell Mum that I've not had sex — though I'd like to! Adrian stops pasting up the wallpaper. What I've revealed of myself is nothing short of dropping a bomb. They'll come round, they'll cope, I tell myself. What's the issue? For godsakes, I'm gay and that's all there is to it. I've spoken about it now, I've freed myself.

The little boy who shares this body, whose parents are on a pedestal, is in turmoil.

— Russell, I don' want this!

Too late, I am a life, not a secret.

NANA FISHER AND my grumpy Grandad live in Pompallier Terrace. I'm unsure whether I like Ponsonby. Everything slopes downhill and the Indian Superette owners sigh disappointedly because I often have only twenty cents to spend on lollies. Nana sends me on shopping errands when she's too busy cooking and cleaning to venture away from the large old villa.

The backyard is fenced in by a gate taller than my four-foot height. I wander out the back admiring rows of sweet peas, where I stand staring into the rich brown soil, lost in a daydream. Often I amble further up the back to trail my legs over the swing at the fig tree. To satisfy my need for freedom and leisure (and to be away from Grandad's incessant growling), I eat the figs — until a queasy sensation turns my stomach.

Tomorrow morning I'll have "the shits". Every few minutes I'll have to scurry indoors to squat on the loo.

TODAY IS A special day for me. I'm catching one of the old yellow buses into Auckland central city with Nana. I'm going with her to clean the movie theatre. I'll even get to see the projectionist check the equipment. Maybe even luckier, I'll see test screenings. I'll sit in the stiff fold-down seats and watch advertisements for an Auckland car dealer roll across the screen. Sometimes I see the first minutes of a film where the Metro-Goldwyn-Mayer lion snarls from inside the logo encircling his head. "Why does it growl before and after movies? How come those curtains pull themselves aside, Nana? Does the man in the box see all the scary movies?"

So — there I sit, watching Nana hoover between the aisles, row upon row of seats. After hours and hours of my running and jumping over seats, Nana signals me from the door to say, "Come on. Home time."

Together we walk up many city roads to the bus depot where Nana buys me a fizzy drink and popcorn. "Are we going to hop off the bus up the road? Are we going to the beer place? Are you an old lady, Nana? Are you thousands of years old? What's that soft smell on your cheek?"

When Nana empties out her pocket lots of lollies fall out. She's been collecting the ones in wrappers from under the theatre seats. Nana will put them all in a jar.

THE BODY SPEAKS:
The head is supported by both hands, the knees pulled up to the chest. This is Nankavelle's posture for keeping sanity. At times, when the Others converse or shout their individual conflicts within his head, the phenomenon becomes unbearable. To hear all of them speaking at once is like a head-on collision. The impact is so overwhelming it feels as though his mind will further fragment. (Sometimes it does, bringing tunnel vision and the fight between emerging selves in their bid to take over the body.) The eyes register colours with a brighter intensity. The inside of the skull feels as though a balloon is inflating between the brain and the cranium. Nankavelle focuses solely on the breathing, maintaining control so that he is not replaced by one of the Others. The concentration is painful for him. Prominent emotions are terror and anxiety. He is determined not to be banished back into the abyss.

I HAVE BECOME unrecognisable to myself at the age of thirteen. Here I am, "The Arrival" — at the Children's Psychiatric Unit, Auckland Hospital.

A sensation within my chest, heart pounding, dizziness — doom! — increases in severity as my mother leads me into the Unit. I'll never get out of here! Walking along the corridor to the nurses' station, I catch a glimpse of a small wooden room with bare floorboards, thickly varnished walls — a "time-out room". Abandonment? Incarceration? There's an outside lock on the door. The sight of that poky little cell fills me with terror.

— Like fuck I'm going in there! an unknown voice hisses through the fragments of my mind. In later years I'm to call him Son of Sorrows.

— Why am I here? What'll they do to me?

— Shut up, Nankavelle. You're a patient now!

I am fighting for consciousness. Several metres along the corridor I "snap to" from an engulfing darkness. Time lapsed, and I'm thinking, What happened? How did I get here? I see nurses in mufti darting in and out of rooms, closing doors behind them. I hear children's voices, some of them laughing, others boisterous, coming from a large room somewhere along the corridor.

Outside the nurses' station Mum and I are met by a balding doctor in his forties who speaks with Mum for a while, in a language I don't understand: "Bit withdrawn, isn't he? . . . Acute . . . psychosis . . . he'll be fine . . . symptomatology . . . residual . . . um, schizophrenia . . . the Professor will be assessing him later on . . ."

As this conversation continues, I stand with my back to the wall, behind my mother, head down, laughing but wanting to cry. Abandonment looms in my mind like a huge neon sign. My body is stiff with fear. I stare at the floor. Amidst all the confusion the Mad-Child surfaces and I cannot understand his thoughts — abstract ideas, colours, shapes and dimensions that seem as though he is speaking in an alien tongue.

The doctor has tried to get through to me but I am trapped behind the Mad-Child who is responding in peculiar body language. He is clearly out of his league. His attempts at communication with the doctor verge on the mental consistency of scrambled eggs.

— He's crazy, the unknown voice whispers through my mind. — You're all fucking crazy! Don't you see, Nankavelle? That stupid child will have us all locked up here in the nut-house forever.

— I want to get out. I want to go home!

— Ah, shut your mouth, Nankavelle, says the nasty voice, and then he's gone.

Throughout this inner exchange the Mad-Child has been in control of the body, hopping from foot to foot and laughing. The only thing I can do is cry inside of myself.

All too quickly Mum's conversation with the doctor is over. She kisses me on the lips and, teary-eyed, she turns her back and walks off along the corridor. By now I have resumed control of the body and I turn my head to one side to watch Mum leave. I sense she is heartbroken. I know she's going to cry when she reaches the car. I feel like crying myself and fear that I'll die. Grieving upon abandonment is like death. As best as I'm able, I compose myself, while in actual fact I'm chipping away inside. Is she coming back? Will the family visit?

The cheery-faced doctor asks me to follow him along a corridor. Once inside an examination room, he shuts the door. I'm scared.

— It's all your fault, pouts the angry teenager whom I can feel sulking. — You got us in here. Your fault, Nankavelle . . .

For a brief moment I hold my breath as the doctor places a cold stethoscope to my chest. He listens to my heart. "Are you anxious?"

"Yes," I reply in a wafer-thin voice. I'm imagining injections and blood tests to follow and this only creates a deeper anxiety.

"That's it. Keep still. Your ears are okay. Can you follow my finger? Good, good. Just follow that finger. That's good," the doctor smiles, encouraging me to relax more as I'm asked to lie down on the examination bed. He presses his fingers into my abdomen. "Good. You're going to the toilet okay? Do you get any headaches?"

His examination is thorough. Now he's unzipping my pants and sliding my underpants halfway down my thighs. I flush with embarrassment and turn my face to the wall. The doctor cradles one testicle at a time in the palm of his hand and rolls each one within his fingers. "Can you cough for me?"

"Yes," I whisper.

"Good." Now he pulls my underpants up over my buttocks. As he zips up my fly he asks softly, "Does anybody touch you down here?"

"No."

"Nobody asks you to touch parts of their body?"

"No." I feel such guilt.

— Liar! hisses an unknown voice, audible only to me.

t w e l v e

M IDDAY. AUDREY IS listening to the radio. I'm seated at the opposite end of the kitchen table, writing a letter to my mother in Auckland. I chainsmoke, look up from my page to hear Audrey ask, "What are you laughing about?"

"Was I?" I'm forever perplexed at how emotions emerge from my body when I have no conscious recollection of expressing them.

"Oh, Matty," she says, "that doctor should do something about your memory."

"Speak for yourself, lady," I tease. "You wander about the house in a flap looking for your glasses, and then find them in your pocket!"

Her eyes glimmer and her face puffs up into fleshy lines around her eyes. She loves me, I can tell — I'm no more odd or mad than she is. My God, we are like an old married couple.

I cock my head to one side, and tune in to Radio Avon's weather forecast. As I do so, something strange happens internally. To complicate matters, my face and body begin to experience alarming physical sensations as if they're no longer mine, undergoing metamorphosis. I am rapidly becoming the intruder inside my own flesh and bone. "Fuck!" I utter. What the hell is happening?

Audrey's face shimmers before my eyes. The radio broadcast decreases in volume, as though from a great distance, inside a tin can. A thousand miles away, across a gigantic expanse of green-topped Formica table, the blurry shape of Audrey is talking to me. "You alright? Matty, speak to me!"

Even more bizarre, my own voice is talking to Audrey through face and lips which don't belong to me. "I'm fine. Just leave me alone." The truth is I am okay. I'm not ill, apart from a wet blanket of impending doom which is seeping into my soul — the body is an organism and I'm the diminishing part of it, shrivelling into that doom which, oddly, now seems as pleasant as an anaesthetic.

As I'm fading from the real world around me, it is the face that causes me deep concern. The face! The warmth . . . isn't mine! My forehead is shrinking, unshaven skin becoming taut, hairless — my skin is softening and the bones are retracting upward into my skull. My chin is growing, jutting forward as an elfin smile puckers onto my fattening lips which are getting broader. This is ridiculous . . . for godsakes, I'm like a man in a horror movie whose bones are cracking and distorting into the face of Dr Jekyll or Mr Hyde!

Now a babbling foreign voice comes from behind me, bypassing me like I'm a detour sign at the crossroads: — Got to letme behere. Got somanythingstodo. Got to runaround tothem an' lookwhile they'renot here.

"Fuck!" It's the only word I can say.

— Mustn't speaklikethat! Speed, speed, gottogo, gottogo. . .

I'm trying to take control of a body which was mine several seconds ago, but the hands are shrivelling, fingers flexing outward, reaching out for my teacup, raising it to a foreign mouth and sipping at the sweet Choysa tea.

Audrey is speaking, her words filtering through to me, smoke through a muslin cloth. I'm barely able to decipher what she is saying: "What's the matter with you? Stop slurping your tea . . ."

"I'm not." But I sense my reply is hardly audible. She must think I'm crazy.

— Speed, speed. Noneofus is crazy. Gottogotoplaces faraway. Noneofusis crazy.

The entirety of my body is still shrinking. Hairs on my chest don't exist. From where I sit in the chair, my feet no longer reach the floor. The sensation of growing smaller, lithe, is the oddest, most confusing experience in eighteen years of life. I am wanting to control this body which I'm fast refusing to accept as my own, to possess it fully as mine, to recognise it as though it were my best friend — mine! How can I even contemplate such a thing when it is an alien skin I'm being cast out of: "My name is Legion, for we are many . . ."?

I try to visualise myself as I am usually, but wait a minute . . . what is Me? The exasperating reality hits home. Who am I?

— Youarewith the restofus . . .

— I need a pink padded cell. I need a doctor . . .

— No, no, you gottobe notloony. You-Us! You-Us!

I may as well be the *Titanic* and sink to the bottom, because the fight is exhausting. I'm so deep inside this abyss that I lack the energy to take responsibility for Speed's body which is now closing the kitchen door, running along the hall, scooting down the street. I have no idea where he is going. I can't see. My eyes are no longer mine, they're his. I can't hear because his ears don't belong to me. I can't feel his nimble little feet making contact with the ground. I am lucky though in one aspect. I'm not totally unconscious and do have a minimal amount of control over this odd situation: while all my senses are paralysed, I'm tuned in to what Speed is thinking. Can he hear what I'm thinking? Is that his name — Speed?

By now I'm completely severed from all physical functions of The Body. Like someone in a coma, I'm trapped in a suspended state, alone with my own thoughts. My body is of no importance, of little relevance, is "someone else's".

How similar this is to death: I've vacated the flesh. Except, in this case, I'm still a passenger in a vehicle somebody else is driving. Do nothing but listen, I tell myself. While afraid I nevertheless remain quiet and learn many things. My God, I've become complicated!

FAINTLY, I HEAR a conversation. I know it's Terry's voice, and judging by the words shared between him and Speed, this is their first meeting.

— Strike a light! Must you hurry, Pal?

— Got togetthere . . . Speed!

— You? Speed?

— Speed! Speed! Got togetthere.

I sense that Speed is quite nervous. He reminds me a lot of Fourteen but is ageless, asexual perhaps? During the takeover of my body I felt my penis shrinking, yet I'm unconvinced that Speed is a child. There is nothing innocent or childish about him, even though the wisdom and intelligence of an adult is absent too. As a self, Speed is more a mechanism, a protective personality who has an urgent need to be constantly mobile, always on the run, anxiety propelling him forward. And horror of horrors, I saw what he was possibly remembering. He was thinking about movement, running after a car which wound around a road, high up an Auckland mountain. His thoughts were jammed — Run, run, run! — and another word repeated, a record stuck in the groove, Cattle — track! Cattle — track! That word seemed to be driving him crazy.

Terry is attempting to hold a focused conversation with Speed. Being strangers to each other, they have to build bridges for communication. Meanwhile I'd like to know where I fit into this puzzle that, somehow, I've become.

I'm aware of where Speed is hurrying the body: along the Avon River. I've made this deducement because I know Terry usually surfaces along the river, hardly anywhere else. He's out again to admire the gardens and character houses across the road from the willow-lined banks. Without him, I couldn't enjoy being out of the house. The mere thought of entering society makes me feel sick and traumatised. That ugly diagnosis haunts me: *Poor social skills . . . antisocial . . . has many fears . . . needs to learn to do some simple, basic things . . . seriously ill, Mrs Nankavelle.* Terry, like Speed, is a bare hope to hang onto.

I've become unique, living lives outside and beyond the limitations some psychiatrists have placed on me. The Others will be my secret, though. To tell the men in white coats of their presence would be a fatal mistake. And so the painful enigma persists: Who are they? Who am I? Can they all hear my thoughts?

— Matthew, we want to live our lives too.

— Where are you from?

I want Terry to say, "Your imagination!" but he promptly tells me he goes back to what he calls "our childhood".

— I can't cope with . . .

— Our presence? One day, pal, you'll see that none of this has ever been *true* madness.

I am no more. Gone. Temporarily snuffed out, a candle flame extinguished.

CONFUSION. THAT FAMILIAR headache.

Where am I? I look around me. Stanmore Road. I'm resuming my own gait and in my right hand is a plastic bag with two ugly goldfish in it.

As Speed descends into the abyss I hear him talking excitedly: — Gotthefish to watchatnight! Got to runhome . . . Gotto hurry. Quick, run! . . .

— Eh? He's not making sense to me.

— Is he in the past? asks a sweet naïve voice.

— Fourteen?

— Yes. Her presence is a welcome relief, as I watch throngs of

Saturday punters entering the TAB. — I'll hold the fish, she says.

Another blackout. When I come to I'm halfway round the river. Terry . . .?

I awaken and find myself beside Audrey on the couch. Apparently we've been watching television. Audrey is in a sour mood. "Why did you scoot out the door at lunchtime? I won't cook for you any more. Where've you been?"

"I don't know."

"Matty, talk to me." She's sad and can't possibly believe that I can only faintly recall being outside the TAB in Stanmore Road. My roller-coaster ride with other realities is killing this woman.

"Leave me alone!" I growl, plagued by unanswered questions. The fish? Where are the fish?

— Gone . . . A new self speaks, a small child.

— Where? Keep speaking, boy. I want to embrace this child.

— In river . . .

Audrey's voice interrupts this inner dialogue. "I'm off to bed. Sleep on your own, Matty."

thirteen

MY GRANDMOTHER DRINKS a lot of lemonade. Grandad refuses to touch the stuff.

It is a summer morning. I stretch my arms and legs, wipe the sleep from my eyes. Through the closed bedroom door I hear the sound of bacon and eggs sizzling in the large metal frypan. The aroma of crisply fried bacon, leaf-tea brewing in a pot, and a portable radio blaring out the Sunday news arouse my senses.

Leaping from bed, I hurriedly dress myself and dash through the living room doorway to greet my grandparents in the kitchen. I smile a wide display of eight-year-old teeth. My grandmother kisses the top of my head and turns back to the stove. I seat myself at the table and self-consciously sip at a cup of tea which waits by my knife and fork. I stir in two hefty measures of sugar while my eyes dart in Grandad's direction. Grandad is wearing tartan slippers and a tatty dressing gown. He lights an Erinmore Flake and, unsmiling, asks," Did you sleep alright, boy?"

"Yes, thank you, Grandad."

— You're so polite, Matthew. Bet you know what's in the lemonade bottle!

— Leave me alone.

My grandmother slips a plate in front of Grandad, then me.

"Mary, come and sit down. Eat with us," complains the old man.

"Ugh, the blasted sink's blocked again!"

"Mary?"

"Yes, dear?"

"Your breakfast's getting cold. Come and sit down." The old man's bushy grey eyebrows cross the bridge of his nose and nearly meet in the middle. Grandmother turns off the tap and seats herself at the table. She smiles at me while Grandad frowns again before tucking into his meal.

My senses drink in all that is around me. The faded linoleum floor, the

ZB news bulletin, jars of preserves stacked neatly in an open cupboard. I long to say something but can't decide how to begin a conversation. I feel semi- at ease in this large old villa on Pompallier Terrace. I'm about to talk when Grandad says grumpily, "Eat your breakfast. You children have got it your own way these days." And his brow creases. I study his chewing and decide that his teeth must be false. "And what about Helen? She doesn't visit much these days . . ."

I'm lost for words. What do I say here?

— He's mean! He's always angry about Mum, whispers an unknown voice. I take little notice as I am too busy nibbling at bacon rind. I'm also waiting for Grandad to finish eating.

— He'll go outside when he stops eating.

— Go away, I order the internal voice.

My grandmother fills the silence. "Are you having a good time at school, dear?"

"Yes . . . and I like my new friends." I reach forward to an empty plate, set the knife and fork down.

Grandad tells me, "Don't cross your knife and fork!" before going into a coughing spasm. I watch him wipe the mucus from his nose and feel hesitant to tell him there's a green bogey hanging off the end of one nostril. Now the old man instructs me to put my plate in the sink and growls, "Why don't you go outside to play? You kids these days don't know how to keep yourselves busy. I keep telling your mother . . ."

"Oh, Fred," groans my grandmother, "Don't bring Helen into this."

"Mary, Mary!" he interrupts. "Our Helen . . ."

"Don't bring Helen into this, Fred," repeats Grandmother, leaving the table in search of a tea strainer. "Go and play, love. Nana will take you shopping later." She opens the back door for me. I wander through to the back yard and make a beeline for the swing in the fig tree.

— I know what's in the lemonade bottle, that voice says again. — Vodka!

f o u r t e e n

A, THE, TO, be, sun, so, we, my, and: fundamental words, but he doesn't understand their meaning. He never reads, never writes. Son of Sorrows calls him "Dumb bum", says that he's as thick as a brick shithouse. He can't think in words. Struggling to hold the simplest of conversations, he grunts, "Ah! Ah! Ah!" He is a miracle in the raw fact that he has been able to survive for so long. I call him the Illiterate One.

His ears ring and he has memories but cannot comprehend the words included with these painful recollections: a slap across the ears and "You're so thick! Stupid little arsehole! Are you listening to me?"

He tries to communicate but is trapped in a world that he cannot understand. What is right? What is wrong? "Ah! Ah! Ah!" he says while his hands defensively cover his body.

Let me explain how the Illiterate One communicates: a violent shaking of his head from side to side means "No". Sudden anger and tears in his eyes convey that he doesn't understand what simple words of English mean. Slapping his own face and thumping one fist into his chest is a frustrated expression of self-doubt. Stamping his feet and rocking his body from side to side means that he cannot verbally express the emotions of anger and fear. Picking his nose and wiping the mucus on his sleeve means he doesn't feel sociable, he's tired and doesn't want to be around people or in public places. Making kissing noises with his mouth is his way of telling another person he feels warmth, love.

Repeated scratching at his head and neck is an indication that the Illiterate One is confused and overwhelmed by spoken words that he can't decipher — as if they're UFOs that have just landed in the middle of the English language. Rubbing at his crotch is an expression of sexual excitement. Banging his head against the wall is a cry of rage and protest which translates, "I don't bloody understand!", while "Ah! Ah! Ah!" can be a description of any subject, thought or emotion.

Frequently his ears ring. He feels afraid, nervous, and in his tiny mind another hand from the past is slapping the side of his head.

He is a young boy who will never grow up, living in perpetual childhood. His shoulders are stooped and a tic causes spasms below his left eye. He is thin and birdlike, does not bathe or clean his teeth because the toothbrush, soap, and face cloth are unfamiliar objects which confuse him. He doesn't comprehend what water is used for.

The Illiterate One has only three functions in his sad little life: eat, sleep, run away from danger.

THE YEAR BEFORE my parents split up — when I was ten years old and a skinny blond-haired child — a teacher at Panama Road School in Mt Wellington left a mark on my life that future years would not erase.

Mr Allan Wilkes was a poor excuse for a so-called Christian. He always had it in for me. He'd break into my peaceful world of creative thought by throwing a piece of chalk at me or he'd slam a leather strap down on my desktop when I slipped into daydreams of books and being a writer.

Two years earlier, when I was only eight, Mr Wilkes called my mother to the school. "Mrs Nankavelle," he said, seated judgementally behind his desk, "your son has a serious problem. He's homosexual."

"So what!" scoffed Mum, "I love my son, and whether he's homosexual or not is none of your business." After telling Mr Wilkes this, my mother left the school feeling very angry. Years later, at the age of eighteen when I came out to my family, she told me of this incident.

Mr Wilkes held several classes. As well as being phys-ed teacher he tutored spelling, and times tables for mathematics: one times two equals two, two times two equals four, three times two equals . . . God, I hate this school. Why do I have to be here? Why does Mr Wilkes stare at me like that? I wish he was dead!

My best friend, Brett, who had a serious heart complaint, was also targeted by Mr Wilkes. This teacher would often make him cry. He disliked Brett because he was excused from playing softball.

One day during assembly Brett began to pick his nose. Within seconds, like a bee homing in on pollen, Mr Wilkes had drawn him from assembly and severely lectured him. I admired Brett for that; I would've gone a step further and outraged this teacher by not only picking my nose but eating it too. I hated that man like poison.

Mr Wilkes (or "Sir" as we were told to call him) often preached to the class. On and on and on he went, "You all must ask Jesus to forgive your sins. Open your hearts to the Lord . . ." And I was thinking: Brett can't open his heart. It's damaged. I even resorted to silent prayer like he instructed us to, but I begged, Lord, please take him away. I hate him! He's always picking on me. Take this mean, horrible teacher away!

Whenever a pupil in our class stepped out of line, "Sir" would either clout the child across the ear or strap the offender in front of everyone else. The latter was a humiliating experience — God, I won't cry in front of the class. I won't! I won't!

In Standard Four, on my final year at Panama Road School, I was to undergo one of the deepest of all public humiliations. Mr Wilkes had asked the class to design a board game on a sheet of cardboard as a way of using crayons and colours, practising ruler measurements too. The entire class worked away for some twenty minutes in silence. "Sir" moved slowly from desk to desk, peering over small shoulders and offering so-called constructive comments and criticism. For several moments he stood staring over my shoulder. I became nervous and struggled to continue drawing. My board game was full of mistakes, smudging, and bleeding felt-pen marks.

"Stand up!" roared Mr Wilkes.

I arose from my seat as quickly as I could, the chair leg grating on the linoleum floor.

"This work is awful. Screw it up — now!"

With two hands I took hold of the cardboard and crumpled it to the best of my ability.

"Over there! Go on, walk over to the rubbish tin and throw it away!"

I did as I was bade, red-faced with shame, and after casting my creative accomplishment into the bin, I walked slowly back to my chair. I hung my head. Surely my game can't be this bad?

"Face the class."

How I wished the earth would open up and swallow me. I stared down at my shoes feeling utterly useless. I'm not going to cry. I'm not! Not in front of all the class.

"Right, repeat after me — head up! — and repeat: 'I am dumb.' Well, go on!"

Body trembling, and shuffling from foot to foot, I parroted: "I am dumb."

"Speak up!"

"I am dumb." The humiliation poured out of my eyes in fresh, hot tears which rolled copiously down my flushed cheeks.

"Sit down. You will do nothing till the bell rings."

I sat down while a voice in my head echoed, Dumb, dumb, dumb. I looked across at my other school friend, Pat. Mr Wilkes had retired to the back of the class and was preoccupied with another student. Pat whispered across the aisle to me, "Don't worry about him."

Forgetting my own humiliation I recalled how often this teacher had strapped Pat in front of the whole class. The voice of Son of Sorrows thundered through my mind:

— Don't worry about the old bastard. We'll survive, kid.

I soon forgot my public disgracing. It was overshadowed by verbal abuse from my thirteen-year-old brother when I arrived home from school: "You little arsehole! You wimp. Poofter! Matthew takes it up the arse, doo-dah, doo-dah!" Sometimes I'd cry, but when Son of Sorrows surfaced my brother had reason to fear. My other self would fight back with legs, fists, teeth, chasing my brother down the hall with a carving knife:

— Kill, kill, kill! Try beating me, you bastard!

f i f t e e n

THE BODY SPEAKS:

Fear means neck and trunk muscles are unable to relax. The eyes are open wide and the muscle below one eyelid has a tic. A sensation of a snake crawling over the skin is what upsets Fourteen and the Children: The Body betrays them, hands shaking, colour draining from the complexion. The calf muscles are tensing, slackening, tensing, slackening, in readiness for the run. And the poor mind . . . it is reeling under memories of violence from long ago. Son of Sorrows is chanting, "Kill! Kill! Kill!"

A DREAM. A small aircraft sits on the tarmac with the door open. An instructor ushers six people into it, myself included. The interior is basic, no seats, ribbed framework supports. The pilot starts the engine and as we skydivers settle ourselves on the floor, our plane taxis to the edge of the runway.

With engines gathering momentum the plane roars along the runway. We are now airborne and the control tower disappears below us. Peering out the dust-stained round window I see the dry Canterbury Plains in full spread. The pilot talks into his radio headset. Our instructor begins handing out huge canvas packs which we painstakingly check. He unfastens the hatch of the aircraft. One by one the other skydivers crawl to the open hatch. After a brief pause and thumbs-up sign, they spill out into the blue emptiness.

My turn has come. I hover at the edge of the hatchway, nervously checking and rechecking my pack.

"Go on, you'll be fine!" shouts the instructor over the noise of the engine and the force of a full wind which is ripping through his hair.

I shiver, looking out into space. The parched earth in small rectangular paddocks is far below. I feel sick.

"Go on!" repeats the instructor before pushing me out the open hatch.

In the savage wind which tears at my canvas suit, I flail my arms. I am spiralling downward, accelerating faster and faster. Above me now I see a perfect star-shaped pattern of the others, arms all linked, floating, safe and beautiful in their chosen freefall.

I start to panic and can't breathe for the wind that is pummelling my falling body. Fear sets in like a cold poultice. I'm going to die. I know this is true because, although I've pulled the ripcord, the parachute trails lifelessly above me, sucked upward by the cold southerly air currents. The earth looms up at an indescribable speed. All I can do is pray, so I cover my eyes with both hands, reciting the "Our Father". Cold-bloodedly I accept my fate. Below me roads are rapidly growing wider. Paddocks rise up at me. They're now on a larger scale. All I can hear is the roar of wind in my ears as it whips my body with cruel bursts of ferocity.

I open my eyes. Twenty seconds to go, I say to myself. The last twenty seconds are hell. My body spins violently and I feel as if my limbs are going to be torn off by the wind. Forgive me my sins, Lord, I say. The impact with the earth hits me. My legs telescope into my gut and my jaw smashes shut so violently that my tongue is severed from my mouth. My arms and head are fractured into little pieces and the pain is unbearable.

My dead body lies in a hollow in the ground. I am no more. What remains is a shattered, blood-soaked heap of brain tissue, multiple bone fractures and gut strewn over the baked Canterbury soil. I float upward. My God, I'm dead, I'm dead! I cry out but nobody can hear me. I'm thinking, Where to now?

ME. ME? WHAT a wretched creature I have become. I am barely thirteen years old. I loathe being a student at Hauraki Plains College. I'm desperately lonely and surrounded by boisterous country kids.

And what am I to them? "A city slicker!". . . "For fucksakes, you arsehole, kick the ball, you shit.". . . "Knew you'd let us down, you're such a derr-brain. Derrr!". . . "There's that crazy kid. Should see him. What a dork. He pretends to type on his desk.". . . "Get away from here, you're not sitting beside me!"

On and on goes the verbal abuse, the sniggering laughter. I can't take much more. I don't want to be here. Leave me alone!

I'm at my desk in the very back row of the classroom. Hot bright sunlight streams through the open windows. Our fat balding teacher stands at the front of the class. As his voice drones on and on, I hear nothing. All I do is imagine, seeing with my mind's eye. I'm looking through the large glass windows and I'm dreaming of peaceful scenarios. I'm grieving for my brother Peter and sister Nicole whom I've been separated from. These thoughts become misery and are launched heavenward — perhaps God will listen to the wishes that rip me apart. Peter is at work now — does he miss me? Does anybody know how I feel? God, please hear me. I hate it here. Let me go to Auckland. Tears roll down my face. I miss Peter. And the feeling hits me. Punch-drunk, I swallow silently, worrying that I may never see Auckland again. I shake, and a lump the size of China clogs up my throat. I must gain control of myself because I fear something awful is going to happen: I'll go crazy, I'll batter the teacher to death and burn down this horrible school, I'll run away from this lonely country life. I hate the other kids here . . . I hate living at that farm! A tremendous pressure is building up inside my skull. My eyes will pop out. I'll die if I have to stay on that farm forever.

My soul is bleeding. It's like having a stake driven through the heart.

There's a gnawing pain on the inside of my chest — which I learn years later in therapy, is the solar plexus reacting to grief. This intense ache is like a mild heart attack and is accompanied by waves of deep sadness, a sense of loss and the unbearable fear: abandonment.

Just when I think I'm about to open my mouth and scream until I've no voice left — a sudden calm washes through me. I take hold of a sheet of paper and feed it through the crack where the wooden desk lid is hinged. I place both hands on the desktop and begin to move my fingers over the imaginary keyboard. Inside my head I'm writing a story about far-away relations: a brother, his girlfriend, a niece, my sister. I'm past caring about what is going on in the classroom. I see nothing but a typewriter.

What do you want to be when you grow up?

A writer, Nana — a writer!

My peace of mind is shattered by the teacher. He has strolled up to my desk and is demanding, "Matthew Nankavelle, what on earth are you doing?"

"Nothing." I'm writing, at least I'm good at something!

"It doesn't look like nothing to me."

The classroom fills with laughter. Simon Cartwright, a loud-mouth kid who's as skinny as a string bean, calls from the left of me, "Ah, he's crazy. What a dork! He's pretending to type on his desktop — ha, ha." The rest of the class bursts into laughter again. I feel like an idiot. They don't understand, *I'm writing*. Why don't they understand? A flush of belittlement heats up my face. I hang my head low and the teacher returns to the blackboard. I refuse to lift my head. I tune out with fresh fantasies about what my brother is doing in Auckland. Every few minutes a lump of soggy paper hits the back of my head.

— They know that I'm different. They know that I like older boys.

— Ah, fuck what they think, Nankavelle! I'll show them. Let them stop *me* from leaving this shit-hole of a school! . . .

— What do you mean?

— Well, you don't think I'm going to stick around, do you?

— You're leaving?

— Too fucking right I am. Let the teacher try and stop me, I'll kill him. I'll kill them all if they dare try and stop me!

— When? I want to go too.

Son of Sorrows lifts his head and gazes out the window to the tennis courts beyond.

— I'll walk through those courts and never come back . . . He turns his head to Simon Cartwright and fixes him with a cold stare. Simon fires another pellet of wet paper. Son of Sorrows vanishes into the dark void where depression sets hard like concrete.

— I'm scared. Suppose the teacher stops me at the tennis courts? Suppose I get into serious trouble? I can't leave. Mum and Adrian will bring me back to school.

— Oh, no they won't! . . . His voice fades away.

I HAVE A recurring dream:

At an amusement park the ferris wheel turns in perfect motion. There's a blue sky above. Big puffy clouds drift across the horizon like gigantic white marshmallows slipping past the fire of a hot, baking sun. People are moving from stall to stall. Mothers and fathers, children and old men. Brothers, sisters, cousins, all with sweet smiles on their Pollyanna faces.

A child, myself in younger years, walks over to a shooting gallery. He places silver coins in the attendant's hand.

With gun in hand he fires shots at a row of moving ducks. A bullet hits one — it falls. Boredom soon sets in. This funpark is far from perfect now. Happiness is unreality. The carousel of fibreglass horses is spinning too fast. The juggling clowns seem demonic beneath their gaily painted faces. My sweet pink candyfloss causes tooth decay.

— I don't like it here. I want to go home . . .

— Shut up and fire that gun!

Another duck goes down. And another. Another. The attendant's face begins to change, reconstructing itself. Face muscles rip and tear, rear-ranging to become a fat middle-aged man. "Do you want to play my game?" he says salaciously. "Go for the teddy bear, kid!" He's leering at me, his lank greasy hair fading to grey. His hands stretch upward to the teddy bear. "You want it, kid?"

"Of course I fucking do!" The bitter voice of Son of Sorrows comes through my child's mouth. A fight begins as I struggle to keep the gun from Son of Sorrows' merciless hands.

The tenth time I dream this scene there is an outcome: The battle is lost and I concede defeat. Son of Sorrows aims the gun at the attendant who runs backwards in fear. Shots ring out. Over and over the slugs fly. The attendant is left dead on the ground inside his shooting gallery and I find myself running from the amusement park, tears streaming down my face. Men and women are running too, like lost souls, for black clouds loom over the park and it rains heavily.

As I run, the voice of Son of Sorrows shouts spitefully within my mind:

I won — I won — I won a fucking teddy bear!

sixteen

MY BROTHER PETER is fourteen and treats me like a baby. He won't take me for rides on his pushbike any more. He and his fat friend Roy have been loaned a 50cc motorbike by the old man across the road. They're racing up and down the street on it. I want to hop on for a ride with Peter but he tells me that I'm a pain in the arse. I miss our push-bike rides and Dad won't have much to do with me now, either.

I spend much of my time playing with my sisters. When I get sick of playing girls' games I go over to Tau Paki's house. I can smoke cigarettes now — Tau and I hide in the shed lighting up his older brother's smokes. Our families will boot our arses if we're caught smoking.

Like me, Tau wants to have a ride on the old man's motorbike. We often sit at the curbside enviously watching Roy and Peter kickstart the old bike. They career along No-Exit Street without any need to wear hel-mets. I've got my old denim jeans on. Tau wears shorts and a T-shirt that Aunty Rona says are his brother's. I can't wear my brother's clothes because his legs are longer than mine and the sleeves on his shirts trail well past my hands.

As my brother careers around the no-exit loop where our house is, I wonder if I'll be invited to go aboard his mate's boat this afternoon. Peter, Roy and their friends smoke and drink beer on board the boat. I know because Tau and I stand on the shore and watch. If my brother is in a good mood he might row me over to the boat in Dad's wooden dinghy, but I'd better not make any smart remarks or he'll tell me to piss off.

The older boys don't like having us around. They tell all us younger neighbourhood kids to fuck off. I've been onto their mate's boat several times, but only for a short while as the older boys want to fish over the side, alone.

Tau and I want to drink beer and smoke. We both hate school and are going to tell our teachers to go and get fucked. We know what fucking is.

Tau's sister says that Bronwyn Ellis down the road is a slut — she's been fucking some of the older boys in the street. I don't want to fuck, I want to catch big fish, drink beer and leave school one day — soon.

Bronwyn has small, peaky tits. All the neighbourhood boys look at her when everyone goes swimming. I've always wanted to see what the older boys often joke about, but I think the masturbation they talk about is when boys rub themselves in their hand and pretend they're lying on top of Bronwyn or other sluts around this street. Roy says that some girls have legs like margarine but I don't get the joke about their legs spreading so easily — I think that's when girls climb over our front gate and have to open their legs and hoist one foot over the other side.

Tau and I know what a cunt is. It's when somebody says you are a real horrible person. I cry, I say that I'm not a cunt because Tau's older sister says it is a girl's place near the piss flaps. Little Tito says you spread tomato sauce on piss flaps, you cook them like stingray flaps. I wonder how a cunt can be like a stingray? If it's food then why does a girl put tomato sauce on them? Tito is a baby, he doesn't know what he's talking about. I reckon that a cunt is a nasty, mean, ugly old person. My brother won't tell me what it means when I ask, and all the older boys laugh at me — what's so funny about being a cunt?

I try not to swear when my parents are around. Mum and Dad say they'll wash my mouth out with soap if I use those words again. Now Mum and Dad are splitting up — what will happen to us four kids? My sisters might move away from the house here, they might forget me, I might not ever see them again.

Mum and Dad both cry a lot. They argue all the time and I feel sorry for my sisters when they start crying too. I won't tell them off for being cry-babies any more.

CHANTELLE'S FRONT LAWN slopes downward. We kids swarm about there for hours, days at a time, in summer. We fight over whose turn it is to replace the kid on the revolving steel seesaw. My legs are too short to touch the parched lawn below. The older kids who are taller, and whose legs can manipulate the height at which we smaller ones are balanced, spin the world around us. I clutch onto steel handlebars and press my thighs as tightly as I can astride the wooden seat which pinches my bum. The yard, the sky, the whole damned street rotates around me. All at once I'm struck with two of the most potent of emotions: pure terror and dizzying heights of joy. I want the world to spin so fast I can't see anything moving. The cheeks of my bum are numb and I'm near hysterical with fear. So afraid that I have become a rigid, steel appendage of the seesaw.

It is this emotion which is all power. I am transformed; I may as well be injecting something into a vein, I'm as high as any drug-induced state of mind. But such potent joy becomes stupidity; the awe and thrill-seeking finishes in woe. Abruptly the speed ends as I'm flung off that crude little seat — smack, bang. My own blood, screams of pain, a mild set of injuries, luckily, but one hell of a headache and a sore lip. A sea of frightened kids hover around me. Any moment now Chantelle's sister will be clutching me to her breast. I'll wilt in her perfumed arms as if I'm dying. She'll kiss my face and call me her "little boyfriend". Before you know it, God will have worked a miracle: the dying will be suddenly healed, then I'll be pushing and shoving and fighting with the rest of them. My turn will come round again.

The babies, the slobbery-gobbed, curly-haired things in nappies, come out to play now. We little kids and older ones ignore them while they play seesaw — as if God himself has just floated down on a cloud, their brown-cow eyes blinking in wonder.

Now the real fun begins. Chantelle has finished washing the car, a gold chariot with fat mags and all the mod cons, the car we all think is the best one in Auckland. She's unravelling the Zoom Slide. That highway of plastic is yellow-striped and made of air-pop bubbles, and it trails down the slope of her lawn. She connects the garden hose to it and squirts a dollop of dishwash liquid on the slide.

By now every kid in the universe has appeared from nowhere, pushing and shoving to get near the Zoom Slide. Chantelle stands by, dishing out rules and regulations: "Give bubba a turn . . . Older kids first . . . Wait your turn . . . No, you've been twice." What a transformation! The silent post-Christmas street is alive with the squeals of delighted children. Little brown and white bodies scurry up the slope, grass clippings thick on our feet. Kids around me are shivering with cold, snotty noses sniff, and large bath towels are draped about our bodies. No sooner do we warm up than our turn to ride the slide has come. Tau goes first each time, slithering at lightning speed down the stretch of plastic, howling "Woo-hoo!" His cheeks are flush with happiness and scrambling back to the place where I stand at the front of the cue, he chimes, "Go, Nannygoat! Go!"

Before me, the highway of yellow stripes slopes away, a downhill torrent of soap-suds and water slosh. My immediate thought is to gather as
much speed as I can. I walk backwards, eyeing Tau who knows that a long
run helps to gather momentum. Like a pro (I must do better than the
older siblings) I take a deep breath, focus all my energy on speed and hurtle toward my target. Just several feet before the plastic I lower my head
and body, arching both arms upward. I dive onto the starting point.
Before I can begin to enjoy the feeling of swift motion, it is all over. Tau
is hooting and screeching with pride and pleasure. What I have is a few
seconds' recall of body impact and then feeling the soggy grass slithering
under my belly. I'm to realise later that such fleeting speed had been
caused by one of the older boys squirting more detergent in the water.

For the rest of that summer and many after, Tau and I would strive to
achieve greater speed on Chantelle's Zoom Slide. Our growing egos would
dictate to us that we must be better than the older boys, and how *dare*
they treat us as "babies"!

I'M ELEVEN YEARS old and living in a new place now, an end-flat of bricks
in Panmure. I go to a new school and I'm quite settled there. Miss Byrd is
a nice teacher. When she reads my notebook from behind me, her tits rest
on my right shoulder. She smells of perfume and smiles all the time. Level
Ten spelling is where I'm at. I take newfound words home and get Mum
to read them out of my notebook. I get most of them right but I can't
always understand their meaning. Mum sits on her bed and defleas the cat
while I chat away about school. She looks tired and has a flagon of wine
beside the bedlamp. I wake up during the night when she cries softly to
herself.

When Dad visits he brings groceries, smiles, but looks sad and I can't
work out why. Sometimes Mum and him argue, so I go off outside and
play with my Matchbox cars. It's summertime because the praying mantis
come out of the bamboo hedge and stick to my forearm. I hate those
insects because they are ugly. I wonder if they bite?

Mum's garden at No-Exit Street is still there and I miss it. When I
visit there Dad is always out front working on the van. I'm upset when
Mum drives through the gates and Dad limps about the driveway wearing
a strange singlet — it looks like fish netting and he has cotton wool stuff
under it. His face and neck are bright red. He looks sunburnt but says that
steam exploded from the hot radiator of the van when he was taking the

cap off. I lie in my bed at night and cry. I think Dad's going to die from those burns. He's been to the hospital and I'm sure they've tried to stop him from dying.

My sister Nicole looks unhappy all the time. I wish she'd smile because I'm glad to be visiting the house at the end of No-Exit Street. Her eyes are full of pain and she says she's being hassled by some of the girls at school. She goes to Otahuhu College. Why doesn't come and live with me and Mum, now that our older sister Cassandra's here too?

My brother will be leaving school. Dad says Peter can work with him, painting cars. He'll be fifteen soon and he's met a nice girl who speaks with a Scottish accent.

As for Cassandra, she goes and stays with Dad, Nicole, and Peter from time to time. She wears her hair in a ponytail and attends a girls' school where the headmistress is a crabby old bat. She came home from school one day to say that a lot of police cars were parked on the motorway. The older girls on the bus told her that a dead man was found under the bridge.

Death is on my mind quite a bit, too. I worry that Mum and Dad will suddenly get old and die. What will happen to us kids? I also feel like I am dying. Inside my head there is a black painful feeling and Mum often asks what I'm worrying about. Maybe I'll be dead soon too but I'm not too concerned as the Bible teacher at school says that Jesus takes the dead people to a wonderful, happy new world. But you have to be good to get into heaven. Will Jesus let me in? Even if I dream about kissing boys all the time? I might be a bad person but I can't help liking the other boys in my class.

I ride my own bike to school now. Dad bought it for me. I like to pedal as fast as I can on the way home from school. I pretend that I'm riding a motorbike as I zoom down the long incline and into my new place, in the end flat.

A best school friend brings packets of chewing gum to class. His father works in a chewing-gum factory. Daryl and I are often seated in the same group of four desks pushed together. We keep a fresh supply of Wrigleys in our mouths, only chewing when the teacher turns her back to write on the blackboard.

Daryl is a hero at school. He's got a long scar running down the inside of one arm, to his elbow. We cluster around him during lunch break and ask how he got the wound. He tells us that the door keys were locked inside his house. He climbed through the window but slipped, breaking the glass and slashing his arm. He needed eighty stitches, so his arm looks like a railway crossing of zigzag thread.

My school work is going well. Mum tells me one afternoon after class that we are moving house, to Mt Eden. I'm excited at the prospect of having a room that won't have to be shared with Cassandra. I'm also sad, because I don't want to leave Daryl behind.

Shortly after Mum packs in her job at the motel we move away from Panmure. I don't like Mt Eden because there are no kids living in my street. I catch a bus to Balmoral Intermediate during the week. Although I'm teased a lot at school I like my teacher who asks the class to write a novel over the first term of this year. I pour all my heart and soul into a notebook sized manuscript — yep, I'm certain that I want to be a writer.

At school I fall in love with a beautiful girl. She's older than me. We go to the cinema in Queen Street. Mum says that I simply have a crush on Anna-Lee. I'm a defiant twelve-year-old and insist that what I feel is love — of course it is, even if Mum's cheeky friends give me a hard time about the girl in my life. Anna-Lee and I telephone each other regularly. I make new friends at school and discover that two boys in my class are the same as me. They are often made fun of, too; called "homos". I very quickly learn what this awful word means. I'm also conscious, when I kiss Anna-Lee on the cheek after dates, that I long to have another friendship as close as ours — but with a boy my own age.

Tau comes to stay for the weekend. We've grown apart. He is fiercely into cars, girls and hero-worshipping an older brother. I, on the other hand, immerse myself in books which I pinch from my mother's bookcase beside her bed. I'm a fan of Harold Robbins and savour the sex scenes, every graphic detail, yet I'm replacing female characters with males. I read Wilbur Smith and another eye-opener, *Papillon*.

My mother drinks wine which she buys from the store several houses away, on the corner of Mt Eden Road and Prospect Terrace. She retires to bed early at night, reads and drinks. I still hear her weeping when the house is quiet each night.

Tau never comes back to stay. He's getting into trouble, a bit like me but on a grander scale. He gets into fights with his brothers and sisters, plays truant and begins thieving from around No-Exit Street.

Just when I can't stand the loneliness of living in this street any more Mum informs me and my sister that we're to move again. I'm delighted at this news, though I have no idea of where we'll be living next.

CASSANDRA HATES TO be called Pippi Longstocking — especially now she's not a kid any more. I still tease her about being freckle faced and skinny with her hair in pigtails. She's left Auckland Girls' Grammar now and has been living away from home. Just for a while, she's settled in again at No-Exit Street with Dad, and she has a job of her own. The Indian man who owns a Superette not far from her home has employed her virtually full-time. My poor sister is being taken for a ride. Most days the Indian man is grumpy and is paying Cassandra one meagre dollar per hour.

When I stay at my childhood home on a Friday night, Cassandra bustles in the front door from work, counting her thirty-four-dollar wage. She is greatly interested in shop work, and later, with the help of the Department of Labour, attends a fulltime retail sales course.

Nicole has also left school. She works a forty-hour week in a typewriter-ribbon factory. Her hands are blackened with exposure to carbon, and she reckons that making typewriter and printer ribbons is a bit of a bore. After several months of work Nicole gets an interview at a cosmetics factory and lands the job. I like to see her breeze through the door on a Friday evening. Her bright blue eyes are full of mischief because once Dad has gone off to visit a new woman in his life, we four siblings crank up the stereo and have a good party.

I love my sisters dearly. Despite their obvious pain about our parents' recent split, the girls are getting on with their lives. Observing my sisters' growth into womanhood, I can only stand in awe of their newly developed adult lives. They now wear make-up and buy themselves skirts and stockings. They smoke and have lengthy telephone conversations with handsome young men who later rumble up our drive on motorbikes.

The house at No-Exit Street on a Friday night brims over with laughing teenagers who drink crates of beer and listen to my brother's Akai Prolab stereo. I snitch glasses of beer here and there, while the occasional mate of Peter's offers me a tote on his cigarette or a swig from his beer bottle. I spend most of these evenings throwing tantrums and then giving in to my belligerent brother who has assumed the role of Father and is adamant that I should be in bed. I'm a teenager now and have a raging temper on me like a psychopath. I'm full of anger at Mum and Dad because I desperately want to grow up and leave home, but I'm still being kept a child.

If there is one moment during these weekend stays at the family house when I'm at my lowest ebb, it is seeing my beautiful sister, Nicole, sitting in the gutter outside crying her eyes out. I have no idea what's wrong with her — except, like all four of us Nankavelles, she has the wish that our parents hadn't found new partners in life. The thought that Nicole is feeling abandoned never enters my adolescent head. She can be so utterly sociable, really happy, and moments later she's a burnt-out empty soul. How am I to know that she's suffering from "clinical depression"?

My brother is a bossy-boots. He's working with Dad in a spray-painting business. Peter's girlfriend, the pretty soft-skinned Scots woman, moves into the house at No-Exit Street. Their relationship seems to be a match made in heaven. They have a wide circle of friends, like to have fun, and jump through the hoops whenever I have one of my tantrums. Peter is sixteen years old now and is to become a father soon. While he and Sheena are love-bugs there's also something sad about seeing two adolescents trying hard to prepare for the role of parenthood. I have no idea of the immense pressures Peter is under. Like him, I think the road ahead will be paved with gold. How naïve we siblings are.

Despite my behavioural problems, I try to envisage some sort of future for myself. I'm already experiencing mental blackouts, saying and doing things which are out of character for me. I'm coated in the newfound shame of realising that I'm probably homosexual. The word itself doesn't mean anything to me, but the more common term "poofter" does. Sometimes, after having a bitter row with my brother, I take off from home, walk the dark streets of suburbia, awakening days later with a foggy idea that, somewhere, I've slept with an older man.

I am unaware that my soul is divided. Vague clues suggest that I'm living in multiple layers of reality. The fragmenting began at age eleven, possibly earlier. I'm being punished by my brother for things I have no recollection of doing. I'm angry and sad, can't understand what is happening to me. By age fourteen it's dawning on me that something sinister is taking hold of my inner world, choking me out like a noxious weed.

Who do I run to?

seventeen

THE PEN IS an extra finger,
    Blue ink surges through my veins,
These words a tide of life . . .
    Coming in, going out . . .
    Receding.

FOURTEEN I MAY be, but I want to write a novel. English is the only subject I've ever enjoyed at school. To think that I was stupid enough to leave that novel behind when I left Balmoral Intermediate. I miss the teacher too, Anna-Lee and other friends. What can I do this weekend other than shut myself in the bedroom, sit at my parents' old wooden desk and draft up a plot in an old school exercise book. I know nothing about writing. My grammar is poor but there seems to be an urgent need to create a different but real world in a fictitious story.

I have no idea where to begin the novel. It's easy to write Chapter One in blue biro, but so difficult to begin the first sentence. Who are the characters? What will they say and do? Suppose the novel never gets completed?

— Like the notebook chapters in Miss Leven's class?

— Eh?

— Yes, I'm here. Does that surprise you?

— Eh?

— Go on, say something, you stupid child.

— Eh? I must be mental, like my brother says. I'm in absolute fear, confusion. — Eh?

— Good God, kid, are you that dumb that you can't speak? Say something to me, boy.

Clearly it's the voice of a woman who is much older than me. She sounds real old. Forty? Her voice inside my head has caused great alarm. I leave the seat at the desk, walk across the room and look behind me.

— I'm inside you, foolish child!

— What do I do? I'm almost crapping myself with anxiety. — What do I do . . . ?

— Keep quiet. That's right, kid. Shut your mouth and say nothing to nobody. The father . . . where is he?

— Eh? I may as well be having a stroke.

— Listen to me, you ugly little sprog! I've unfinished business with the father.

— Yeah? I feel battered about the head with a sledgehammer.

— So keep out of the way.

These secret voices seem so bizarre that I daren't even tell God, daren't even pray any more as I was taught at primary school. For now this new oddity of my life will have to become the deepest secret, locked within me along with other unmentionable relics from the past.

Keeping them secret isn't as simple as it may seem: I can't cope, so I retreat somwhere inside the black void of time. No doubt I'll reawaken at some point in the future . . .

Click. The biro is hitting the desktop. I'm gone; let the Mad-Child take over. He's pacing the room and is both angry and bewildered. He hears the sound of my brother and sisters laughing along the hall where they are drinking in the kitchen. Mad-Child opens the bedroom door. He sprints down the hall and slams the bathroom door shut behind him. He's standing on the edge of the bath, the shower track digging into the arches of his feet. Confused, he stares into the mirror, examining his face. Wonders what is real. Worries that he, as a self, isn't actually real. The words, "Go! Go! Go now!" spring from his mouth. A moment later, he too has retreated into the abyss.

Son of Sorrows is standing there. He has hold of my father's old razor blades. — Kill you, Nankavelle! he's saying as I surface again to see my own face in the mirror. I look down at the basin which is spattered with fresh droplets of blood. My fingers are bleeding. — Should stop you writing, fuckwit! His voice fading into a pool of anxiety which washes over me. In panic, I turn on the taps and attempt to flush away the blood. Red ribbons of my life are swirling down the plughole. At this moment I feel utterly desolate. The more I try to get rid of any trace of blood the messier the basin gets. I'm worried that my brother might bitch at me for being stupid enough to cut my fingertips. He'll probably take one look at Dad's razor and say something like, "You'd better clean that up. Anyway, you're too bloody young to shave that bum-fluff on your face. Stupid poofter." I can't bear such cruel taunts. I could easily snap and fly at him in a state of rage. I'll scream and perform; make him sorry for calling me such derogatory names. Suppose I killed him? I have to be ultra quiet, so I pad along the hall as noiselessly as possible. I bind toilet tissue around my fingers and sneak back into the bathroom.

Fresh tears are spilling from my eyes. What have I done? All four fingers on both hands are stinging and the loo paper is drying into the cuts. I clean the basin as best as I can. Panic increases when I hear the kitchen door opening. Moments later my brother is pummelling on the door.

e i g h t e e n

THE BODY SPEAKS:
The Mad-Child suffers terribly with vertigo. His visual perception of reality is limited by the fear of seeing something he doesn't want to see. The eyes close frequently. Everything is frozen into an upright posture to prevent Son of Sorrows emerging and taking revenge for making the child body a laughing stock. To the medical profession this appears to be a trance, has even been diagnosed as a temporary form of catatonia. Trapped in this state, Nankavelle is unable to activate the vocal chords and report, "We seem rigid because if Son of Sorrows gets out all hell will be unleashed." The Mad-Child stares out through unblinking eyes and sees the vista as bright scarlet red. Some doctors speak about Nankavelle as if he isn't present in the room, and all the while he is thinking from his imprisonment of flesh: If only you knew that I can hear every word said about me.

"*I FELT SO* degraded. I felt like a lump of shit, so small, so useless and ugly in that house." I am remembering.

"Why? What was said?" prompts my psychologist.

"Fucking little mongrel. Poofter. Froggy-eyes. Ugly. And there were other names, degrading words."

"Such as?"

"I don't want to repeat them,.."

Ralph inhales deeply. His eyes are watering. "Sticks and stones may break my bones, but words can never hurt me."

"Mmmm." I shy away from further discussions about hurtful names. I suppose that Ralph is right.

AUDREY IS STANDING in the open doorway to what was once our room. I've made the biggest mistake of my life. I should never have entered into an affair with her. She the older-and-should-have-known-better, and I the kid-who-needs-to-grow-up.

Strange! The relationship was built on the sandy foundation of needs, each of us wanting to be loved, protected, never to be alone or lonely. The social disgrace we'd encountered along the way had been rebuffed with our disclaimer: "Who cares what the neighbours think!" (Easier said than done, eh!)

My bags are packed and a car horn toots outside. I'm crying, she's crying — finito! We both give an accusing you-hurt-me stare and it's all over. I'm single, is hesitantly acknowledged within me.

— You are definitely gay, admit it . . .

— Go away, Russell!

AUDREY BOARDS A Kaikoura-bound train. I hug and kiss her at the central railway station. Tears fill my eyes when the carriage pulls away from the platform. I wave my hand as Audrey blows a kiss through the window. I read her lips above the noise of the train. "I love you," she's saying and my heart melts.

Our relationship has come to an end. I knew this some months ago. I've been reluctant to move out, but the reality of the situation is hitting home: my other self, Russell, is gay and I am too. God, I'm confused. Were the doctors right? During my psychological assessment at Edwin Hall Clinic in Sunnyside Hospital I'd been told, "You are experiencing a sexual identity crisis." I'd felt insulted at such a conclusion. Weren't the doctors really saying, "You're sexually immature — grow up!"

Three and a half years with Audrey. One day soon I'll be moving out of her house. I'm excited but also apprehensive about my future. Perhaps I'll rent a flat, write my short stories and make new friends? She wants me to go . . . I hope we can remain good friends.

I EXPRESS TO Ralph the anxiety that I'm different — not normal.

"What *is* normal?" he asks.

Lost for words, I revert to old negative messages of self-doubt. I stake my claim to a category into which I've been so neatly slotted: "How would I know? I'm supposed to be schizophrenic."

"Bullshit," my psychologist says. "You're depressed. Why?"

Because I'm confused by all this division inside me. I'm also paranoid about opening my mouth, in case the words "we" or "they" may slip out.

Ralph sighs, "You don't have to talk to me. You can pretend to be crazy if you like — if that's what you want."

"I can't . . . I can't . . ."

"Go on, say it."

"I *can't* . . ." What I'm trying to say is that I can't find normality, there is no peace of mind. A new self, Trevor, emerges from the shadows of my inner world, and behind him, Son of Sorrows is waiting to strike. I'm sucked into the dark vortex again.

A DOUBLE LIFE, that's what I'm leading. By day the Mad-Child lives up to that dusty old diagnosis of schizophrenic. By night I'm in control and roam around the rain-drizzled streets. Knocking on the door of a man whom I've only just met. Drinking his coffee. Listening to his confession that he's worried the rugby team are figuring out that he's gay. Taking off my clothes and slipping into bed beside him. I never see his body naked as we have sex with the lights out. Another coffee, a cigarette, a kiss at the door, and I slink home in the early hours of the morning, the tomcat who's sated his sexual appetite.

Within minutes of slipping the key into the lock, Trevor has surfaced. He makes black coffee, slips a sheet of A4 paper into the typewriter to write about my sexual episode with the rugby player. A chapter which explodes the myth of gay stereotypes. Gay men aren't pink and flowery — they even play rugby!

"HELLO. GOOD TO meet you." Ralph acts as if he's greeting another person rather than me. Why is he shaking my hand?

"What?" I ask. "Have I just arrived?"

"Didn't you just come in?" His eyes scan my face. I presume he's waiting for my response.

— If I didn't come in through the door, well then, who did?

— Snow White and the fucking seven dwarves came in! Jesus, Nankavelle, your mind is like a sieve.

"Ralph . . ." I'm hesitant to ask what appears to be a vacuous question. "How long have I been here?"

Sitting down, my therapist laughs. "You've just this moment walked in." I sense that he's trying to lighten the moment.

"Why did you . . ."

"What? I can't read your mind, Matthew."

I interrupt with a groan of dismay. "Oh . . . nothing," I say, sitting down opposite Ralph who smiles.

"Your life is crazy at the moment. But you're not insane. You're here, in part."

What does he mean? Am I the crazy one? Or is he?

— If you ask me, all men are crazy. "Bastards!"

"Who are the bastards?" Again Ralph lightens the moment: "I'm not a bastard," he laughs. "You can trust me."

I shake my head. "Bastards? What are you talking about?"

The man whom I've come to call "my therapist" has grown serious now. "Didn't you hear what you just said?"

Rising from my chair, I turn my back on him for a moment. I walk over to his wash basin and check my face in the mirror. Something's not right. I face my therapist and feel shamefully naked as if a raw nerve has been exposed.

"Something's wrong!" I touch my face and brow with both hands. "I wake up from a black emptiness and find myself here in your office. I find freshly made coffee beside my bed. I forget where I live, I walk past my place and wonder which house is mine."

"You do?"

"Well, I think so. Oh, what do I know? Damn these blackouts!"

"Blackouts? You mean lost time." Ralph adjusts his bifocals.

"Blackouts? I don't have fucking blackouts." Son of Sorrows has taken over my body. Vaguely, I'm aware that I'm standing behind him, seeing nothing but fog. I can only hear the following conversation:

"Who," says Ralph, seizing the moment, "are the bastards?"

Son of Sorrows' eyes narrow, his chin juts outward, as violent thoughts charge through his mind. "You're all fucking bastards. Men! You're all the same. What are you going to do? Fuck children like *all* the men in the world?"

"Like who? I'm not one of those men . . ."

"You know who!" He is thinking about Uncle Nankavelle.

"Don't play games with me," Ralph is saying.

"Is that your fucking style? I should've . . ."

"You wanted to kill your abuser. What stopped you?"

Glaring at Ralph, Son of Sorrows is gone in a split second. I'm left feeling puzzled. I sit nervously in my seat, wondering why I slipped into the abyss and could hear such venom pouring out of my mouth. A mouth different from my own.

"I heard all that, Ralph."

"Where did you go, Matthew?"

"Go? I don't know."

My therapist looks bothered. "Matthew," he says, "you're not alone."

"I know. But I'm so confused."

Ralph changes the subject. "You could keep a diary. Write down what has to be done each day, and you may find out where you go . . ."

"But I tried that," I protest, "and the diary disappears."

"Mmmm," comments Ralph, "like time."

"Yes," I agree.

"Like clothing and books."

"Maybe I'm possessed?" I try to make a joke of it but it doesn't lighten the heavy load of anxiety weighing me down.

"'My name is Legion and we are many?'" Ralph laughs in return. Yet I think he also intends the statement to be serious, to touch some part of me.

"Yeah!" I giggle, not touched anywhere; understanding nothing.

— Don't fucking trust him! Son of Sorrows is warning. He has a cock, remember!

MY FAVOURITE SHIRT, buttons torn off, lies crumpled on my pillow.

"Who did that?" I demand. Oh, this is stupid. Who did that! For god-sakes, I simply don't remember. I pick up the shirt and retrieve a small piece of torn paper in the pocket. It reads, "Adam" and a phone number.

— You went to a man's house . . . Fourteen has surfaced.

— When? When, Fourteen!

— Are you going to call him?

— Of course I am. Did I sleep with him?

— You had coffee with him and caught a taxi home.

— When, Fourteen?

— Yesterday. Night time. You mad at me?

— No!

I feel her shiver as she fades into the abyss.

n i n e t e e n

THERE'S A FOX in my mother's wardrobe. If I drape it around my shoulders, will it savage me? Its eyes are cold glass. The mouth is open, baring long white teeth. Mum and Dad are out this evening, which is why I'm here ratting through the dark expanse of a clothing-stuffed wardrobe. My sisters and I are playing dress-ups. I wear a fake fur coat. It's a shiny pearl colour and reeks of perfume. I always wear my favourites: Mum's calf-high boots which are tanned brown leather and, of course, they come right up over my knees.

This game is fun. I get to watch Cassandra and Nicole trying on different scarves and plastic 'sixties bangles that clatter about their skinny wrists. I have no desire to be a woman. The role I play is based on fantasy about importance. I'm wearing fur, leather boots and a dash of perfume, therefore I am somebody who is successful.

The girls play Abba records. I'm not allowed to touch the stereo because my hands are unsteady and I might scratch the records.

With hairbrushes held like microphones, we mime, "'I do, I do, I do, I do!'" and my role here is dual. I'm Benny or Bjorn; sometimes I'm Agnetha. There's a definite aura of security which washes through me whenever I'm playing dress-ups. The after-scent of Mum's presence and the softness of fur makes me languid. I put the fur coat in my bed and sleep on it. Like a Linus blanket, it's far superior to sucking one's thumb.

Eight years old, and Dad is starting to worry about me. I'm not an aggressive child but flirt and get preoccupied with any woman who will let me sit on her knee: aunties, friends of my parents, grandmothers, I cuddle into big breasts, small breasts, bury my face into well-perfumed necks and soak up all the attention. I cry easily, daydream literally every hour of the day. I shut myself indoors where I leaf through Wilbur Smith novels. On some occasions I fold and sew notepads into small books, fill them with Wombles cartoon stickers, and write some text under them. I love pens and pads and paper clips. On rare occasions Dad reluctantly takes me fishing. I love to steer the boat, fantasising to my heart's content that I'm on the rocky shores of Rangitoto. A self-obsessed child I'm becoming. The voices in my skull now identify themselves as "he" or "she" and speak of me as "you". I shudder to hear them say "Us". I'm crowded out of my own head by others who taunt and hurt me with cruel words and threats. I can rage like a volcano and seemingly recover from the tantrum moments later, denying their existence. "I didn't do that," I claim while a voice is chanting inside me, "Liar! Liar! Pants on fire!"

I'd like to cuddle up to my father, tell him that I love him, but he's too busy downing whisky and tuning in to the horse races at Ellerslie.

If I'm lonely then I compensate for it: I spend hours in my sisters' bedroom playing with Barbie dolls and watching water dribble out of Wendy Doll's steel pipe vagina — such bliss, a doll that really piddles!

I'd be out skateboarding or fishing if my brother would let me tag along with his pre-teen friends.

Awful things happen in the house because I cause them to occur. It's utter delight to see my eels slithering about the wet sheets in the laundry tub — "See what me and Tau caught? Big eels, eh!" Sinks are blocked and overflowing because the shavings from my potato-head men have clogged the plughole. A trailer full of grass clippings is set on fire after I tossed one of Dad's cigarettes into it. And then playing fireman with the hose, feeling scared because I started the fire.

WHAT'S HAPPENING? TOO late. He's switched on the light, is pulling my long hair back and tying it in a ponytail. He's forcing me out of existence — for now, at least. He's opening the bedroom door and, as the hallway grows darker, I'm sinking further into the abyss. I'm gone, into anaesthesia, the hallway walls and carpet fading from view. Through a fog I hear him opening the dining room door . . .

— A lot to get through, he's telling me, and right now, in the late hours of night, I'm behind him, hearing, thinking — then, blank. Trevor Daniels is seated at the oak dining table. A portable Olivetti clatters to life under his nimble fingers. He's writing about my life, a case history of what it is like to be homosexual. He's got the "inside story" on me and is compiling all his research. It is a lengthy manuscript where the pros and cons of sexual liberation are argued: religion versus homosexuality with the real "immoral acts" being homophobia, discrimination and gay bashing; Chapter Four, Exploding More Myths; Chapter Eleven, Coming Out to Family. Included are several pages of transcripts from an interview with Ralph on the origins of homosexuality.

Trevor's smoking tailor-mades and guzzling coffee around the clock. The typewriter is in a flurry of activity for eleven hours. Daylight arrives and he yawns. I surface from the abyss, my eyes burning through his exhausted stare.

— I've finished, he sighs.

I look around me. The curtains have been drawn and on the table is a wad of typewritten pages. I pick up one and read it. My life. Why?

— You're not to concern yourself with these. Trevor's left hand takes the page from my right hand. I've recently learned that two selves can inhabit my body, simultaneously possessing a part of it each.

— Up all night? Perhaps I should slap my own face, pinch myself to make sure the stack of paper before me is real.

— Eat something. Look at the clock.

— I can't read it. Anxiety sets in like cold congealed soup.

— Ten thirty-four . . . am. You must eat. Feed The Body.

I reach behind my head and peel Trevor's elastic hairband away from his ponytail. Who wrote all night? You, Trevor?

— Yes.

And I almost despise his indifference towards me. He's arrogant and seldom speaks to me. His long conversations, fuelled by my therapist's interest in his life, are beyond me.

— You needn't think that. Ralph is seeing *you* at eleven.

I feel stupid, small, insignificant. A likeable man inhabits my body, while all I can do is hope that Trevor will be gone forever, soon. It's a bad dream; I'll awaken in my bed and laugh to think that these other selves are the product of my brain while in REM. Am I jealous of Trevor's freedom to write?

Another time lapse. Who's there?

A long silence is followed by a new voice, a monologue of disconnected sounds, a fractured speech pattern:

— T-T-T-To-To-day-day, I-I-I-I-I . . . g-g-go . . . to-to . . . R-R-R-R-al-al-ph's . . .

— Ralph's session? Why?

— C-c-cold w-w-w-w-w-aater . . .

And now Trevor Daniels is mediating, like a para-brain, a shining beacon of knowledge. And, to my utter astonishment, he knows so much of our lives.

— You don't need the memory. Go, I'm telling you, Stutter-Mouth! Go!

As Stutter-Mouth fades away in a cloud of fear, he transmits the memory to me.

— You don't need to remember this, Nankavelle!

It's raining. I can feel the sensation of intensely cold water from a concrete fountain in Mission Bay, mid-winter 1980. There are two drunk men, and I've also been drinking beer. The fear and rage mount as two supposedly good friends chase and capture me, dragging me to the fountain, hauling me up by the legs and arms, swinging my body. "One, two . . . three."

"Let me go, you bastards!"

"Four . . . five."

I splash into the water. When I stand up I'm cursing at the two men who're beside the fountain, laughing. "You fucking bastards. You f . . ." Stepping out, I turn my back on them and stomp along the road in a blind rage.

"Come on," calls the elder one. "Come with us. I'll shout you a hamburger."

"Bastards!" I call over my shoulder. I'm deeply humiliated. The Auckland sky is cloudy and a sea breeze blows in from the sea. I walk for hours, the voice of Son of Sorrows repeating in my head: — Kill them. I will . . . kill the bastards. I will.

I don't know how I got here but I find myself standing on Bastion Point, the waterfront below me. I'm blue with coldness, still dripping wet, and my faded jeans chafe the inner thighs with each step I take . . .

And here I am, 1988, twenty years old, and standing in the dining room, shaking with cold. The presence of Trevor Daniels is fading. I can only hear his voice in my head now:

— Just try and forget that memory.

— But who was that?

— His name's Stutter-Mouth. Don't deny his existence . . .

— But he's so *young*.

t w e n t y

AFTER A DISASTROUS attempt at flatting by myself I've gone to live in an old character house with Mum and Adrian who returned from Auckland some months ago.

One morning I find a Situations Vacant advertisement in the community newspaper. As I read it through, ambition stirs within me. They're inviting submissions from those with journalistic talent. Grading is unnecessary as full training is to be given on the job. My heart sings, This is my chance!

— You're destined to be a novelist. Leave non-fiction to me.

I cringe to hear Trevor's words, but he's right, fiction is more my forte, though I'm a writer with little confidence. I'm stumbling along blindly with many creative ideas for the great Kiwi novel. I'm a novice with a lot to learn. Nevertheless, I fool myself that perhaps I could succeed with journalism. Factual writing? Why not give it a try?

Telephoning the editor, I enquire about the position and express a strong interest in the paper. I'm full of hope, certain that I can learn and that the job will lead to other things. I couldn't imagine a more perfect working environment: desk and typewriter; following leads, doing interviews, keeping deadlines. Yep, I've got what it takes, I can do this. Bluffing my way, I convince the editor to look over a folio of my writing.

I have two weeks to collate samples of my work, to retype and edit, before I present them to the editor. I labour over thirty pages. My confidence increases. A phone call comes from the editor saying he's going away for a week and would like to see my work when he gets back. I'm on cloud nine, picturing myself as part of the newspaper scene, a tornado of creative output, in corduroy trousers, puffing on cheap cigarettes and meeting deadlines with time left over to twiddle my thumbs. Ten years on: my own column?

As the tension mounts I polish my scripts to an insane degree where I'm convinced that the job is already mine. Journalism? I can do it!

After two weeks go by I pick up the telephone and ask for the editor. An unfamiliar voice comes on the line.

"Hi," I say, "it's Matthew Nankavelle calling. You're not the person I spoke with a fortnight ago . . . Oh, I see . . . Well, Michael Gideon asked me to prepare samples — I'm sorry? . . . About the advertisement . . . Yes . . . you're serious? Oh, I see." Emptily, I walk away from the telephone, my heart in my mouth. I'm leaning against the hallway wall crying my eyes out.

My mother appears from her bedroom. "What's the matter, love?"

After several minutes of weeping I gather myself together. "They've had a change of editor and employed a sixteen-year-old trainee . . . "

"Oh, love," Mum says, placing a hand on my shoulder. "Perhaps you expected too much?"

"Mum, they didn't even get to see my folio . . . "

"You've worked so hard. Look at you. You're worn out . . ." She smiles at me, her eyes full of concern. "You'll make it, love. You will."

How do I even begin to explain to her that I'm not the one who's been up all night writing? I'm not you, Trevor. I'm no part of you, Daniels. All I've ever wanted in life is for my writing to progress into eventual publication. Twenty years old. My God, I've failed.

— This is a process you must endure.

— Trevor Daniels, I hate you.

"Mum?"

"You'll get there. Don't give up."

"I've failed, Mum." Fresh tears. I just want to sleep, and wake up to a brighter world where I'm the sole inhabitant of this body which has become "Our body".

A FRIEND OF my mother's comes to stay. Deborah is a quiet, shy girl of eighteen and has a ten-month-old daughter, Jodie. Mum has always been willing to help those around her in need. Deborah has broken up with a violent man, left a small rural township, and is in Christchurch to look for accommodation.

Jodie is a sweet pea, all smiles, a good natured kiddy. I'm such a fool and so lonely that I fall in love with them both, mother and daughter. Deborah and I spend much of the day together, grocery shopping, scanning the "To

Let" columns in the newspapers. We have so much in common because we are both bookworms, smoke the same brand of cigarettes. Often a good laugh is shared over late-night television and hot sweet coffee.

My mother is glad that I'm company for Deborah. Adrian, my stepfather, is away down south, so Mum busies herself with gardening and other household chores. "Adrian will be home soon," she says with sadness in her eyes. Meanwhile she has four more days to wait before he visits for a weekend.

Deborah is there for Mum. While Trevor Daniels spends the morning writing, the two women bus into town, shopping and choosing clothes for Jodie from secondhand shops. I notice how my mother flowers in the company of another woman — she's relaxed, assertive — I guess she's missed woman to woman interaction. With me, Mum has a strong-minded man, older than The Body looks, and calling himself Trevor Daniels.

I, on the other hand, spend my days muddling through waking hours wondering where the hell so much time is going. I reluctantly resign myself to the division of the inner me, trying to present to the world a brave, if not defeated, face. I, Matthew Nankavelle, who is sinking to the bottom of a deep pit, have my moments. My self-esteem is threadbare and I cry frequently when I'm alone in the nocturnal privacy of my bedroom.

I'm feeling lost now that Russell has faded, no longer existing — or rather, I've absorbed him, which means I'm having to cope with the disgraceful reality that, yes, I'm gay. (At present I'm beginning to express myself through Trevor Daniels' heterosexuality. When confronted with the truth, I say, "Yes, I'm bisexual." Trevor becomes an ally, keeping the secret.)

MY OTHER GRANDPARENTS live in Point Chevalier, Auckland, in a modest house with a beautiful garden on a quiet street. I love my grandmother very much. She is a rare kind of person — a spirited woman with a mad passion for cats and an impressive orchard out the back of the house. She sings non-stop, her high-pitched voice wafting out of the kitchen and down the hall to where I sleep. "Tra-la-la-lahhh," she trills, and she can be heard clattering about with pots and pans.

How best can I describe her calibre? Sunlight breaking through upon the day-to-day grey terrain of suburbia? A lover of good food and children? A family icon? Sweet, all bosom and maternal cooing and fussing? I adore her.

And my grandfather? I don't quite understand men, their camaraderie, cold beer and insatiable appetite for private sexist jokes, but "Dick" (as my grandmother calls him) has an aura of his own. Too busy to rest when there is work to be done, a strong, wiry man with a well-seasoned heart — sprightly and energetic until a respiratory ailment eventually reduces his zest for life. Poor lungs maybe, but they certainly don't prevent him from taking his daily walk around the neighbourhood!

Beverly — my father's sister, who lives with Nana and Grandad Nankavelle — is the strongest link within our family chain. Working daily, virtually fulltime in a financier's office in Karangahape Road, she returns home in the evenings and helps out with meal preparation, and often, supervises many grandkids. Seldom does she complain, yet even as a child I can sense that family duties and responsibilities take precedence over her own life. She tends lovingly to my childhood needs while, again, I'm thinking, Where is Aunty Beverly's boyfriend? How fortunate I am to be cherished by her — me, the sensitive, day-dreaming boy of eight years old.

When I'm staying with Nana and Grandad I discover all sorts of exciting things about the atmosphere within that wonderful home. To sit close to the kerosene heater and watch *Coronation Street* on the old black and white television — that's a treat in itself. I'm transfixed by the portrayal of an adult world I'm lucky enough to be viewing. What warmth there is in being nestled into Beverly's upper arm, drinking my cup of never-too-sweet Milo, deciding how best to make the ginger crunch last forever . . . and wondering, will I, too, be an actor when I'm older? A fireman? A policeman?

After my curiosity's been quenched for another night by the drama of Ena Sharples lashing out at another unfortunate youngster on "The Street", it's bedtime. I'm taken to the bedroom at the end of the hall, kissed, wished "Sleep tight!" — and the light is switched off. I'm perpetually afraid of the dark but manage to lose myself in whimsical fantasies of hosing out fires and climbing ladders.

I stay awake as long as I can, sometimes hearing Aunty Beverly cough in her bedroom. My mind visualises an oblong tin of Strepsils but I still don't sleep. I'm eager for the chiming clock above the kitchen table to strike midnight, GONG! GONG! GONG! . . . and I'll silently count from one to twelve.

Morning must have arrived because Nana is standing in the room, opening the venetian blinds on the window opposite my bed. She hears me stir and stretch my arms, and offers me a warm cup of Milo. I emerge from the haven of blankets and stumble down the hallway where Nana whistles about the kitchen. Grandad's radio is broadcasting the 7 am news bulletin from the other side of the table.

These are the ordinary events typical of the New Zealand lifestyle of the seventies, but such warmth cannot easily be forgotten.

DEBORAH AND JODIE have stayed here with Mum and me for almost two weeks now. Trevor packs away the portable Olivetti halfway through one afternoon. He spends most of the remaining day joking and laughing with my mother's friend. By this time they are exchanging longing looks and the occasional kiss. After a wearisome afternoon Mum goes to bed to read. Deborah and Trevor have shut the lounge door. They're trying to have sex on a camp stretcher and what follows is a lot of hilarity, frustration, aggravation and a cigarette break because "This bed's going to collapse". What should be spasms of pleasure are near-convulsions of laughter. Deborah is deeply embarrassed and frightened that our laughing is going to wake the baby, who is cocooned in a cot blanket on the couch.

— Trevor! You can't do this.

— Why not?

— My God, this is unreal. You're trying to have it off in my body. And all I can think about is . . .

Before I complete the sentence he's saying, — Jesus, trust you! That's because I'm allowing my own fantasised images of sexy men to flood into his thoughts. This is a successful attempt at revenge. Well! I wanted to visit the rugby player.

— The gay one who does it with the lights out? Nankavelle, you are crazy!

Nevertheless I'm contentedly ruining Trevor's moment of thwarted passion even further. He's becoming angry, now that our body's erection is down. I leave him, escaping into the safety of the abyss.

What ends here begins here: Trevor has entered headlong into a relationship with Deborah. The sun may as well shine out of her, she's his ideal dream: love and fatherhood.

What he fails to realise is that she is on the rebound and isn't attracted to an intelligent creative man like himself; she is a bored girl who desires love for the wrong reasons. What seems perfect is to be brought into the light, warts and all.

MY MOTHER DRIVES them to the remote green hilly township of Parnassus, several hours drive from Christchurch. Deborah and Trevor have talked most of the week about living together. Jodie has taken a shine to her Mummy's new man and has started to bond emotionally with Trevor who has become less of a stranger to her each day. He feeds her, picks her up when she cries. How can such an adorable baby not smile to see a male influence in her life again? Trevor's downfall is that he is a natural-born father, is wonderful with nieces and has time for kids — all good qualities for paternal commitment, perfect recipe for a broken heart.

— Shut up, Nankavelle, he tells me. What do you know about it?

— She wants a father for Jodie, I'm quick to reply.

— So?

— Love is blind. I know I've overstepped the mark, but nothing can deter Trevor from the truth which lies in wait, a lion in the grassy green woods, claws flexing, ready to leap out and mortally wound.

Mum says nothing, smiles, drives away tooting the horn. Trevor looks about him at miles of rolling paddocks and an old weatherboard villa creaking under the strain of a gusty wind passing through the wide open spaces.

Deborah leads the way into her house, Trevor carrying the baby into the spacious living room. Both are worn out and Jodie starts to grizzle.

T H E   B O D Y   S P E A K S :
Disappointment can often take on physical manifestations. Nankavelle has learnt that "patience" doesn't mean wait, it means to be kept dangling on a string. The Body loathes this waiting period. It wavers in expectation while the Others make ready for the promise which will, quite probably, never be lived up to by those who claim to be reliable: an absence, or "Sorry, forgot to call and cancel". The gut sags, feelings of deflation and despair, while Nankavelle flagellates himself: "I should have known!" The mouth slackens, the eyes half-close, sleepiness ensues — the wait has exhausted him. His life is full of unreliable people.

THE MAGIC HAS gone. Trevor Daniels is living with a woman who is no longer interested in books or intelligent conversation, let alone sex. The warm eyed, silk haired Deborah is rapidly becoming a super-bitch. She's flipping out to realise that Trevor is unfamiliar male territory. He's not her usual boozed, homicidal maniac who beats her and rejects her child. Instead, Trevor is all goodness, warmth, security. He's even beginning to assume the role of husband and parent. During the cold wintry mornings when the baby screams from her cot and her mother returns to sleep, Trevor lights a fire, feeds the little girl, clothes her. The baby is bored; Deborah treats her as merely something to be fed, cuddled, and banished to bed.

Trevor hesitates to complain to this woman who he's not so much in love with any more. He believes she is going through a bad spin. Unfortunately, Deborah is no phoenix arising from her ashes. The situation worsens. Trevor is unaware that the young woman feels trapped. What she gravitates towards is violence, to be rolling drunk and have some shaven-headed moron slip his nazi tongue down her throat.

— Bugger this, I want out! I tell Trevor.

— So what if she threw a jar of jam at us? Trevor is making any old excuse, swallowing his girlfriend's line about Pre-Menstrual Tension.

— Trevor, I say, as tactfully as I can, she's not attracted to you. She's running scared.

— These problems can be sorted out. You're such a bloody pessimist, aren't you, Nankavelle!

I reject this. I'm gay, eh. Where do I fit into all this?

All he can say is, You don't!

I retreat to the quietest part of the house, feeling strained because Deborah's parents are coming around later today. In dread I lie on the bed listening to the anaesthetising sounds of rural life. The rain has eased and all I can think of is being back home in Christchurch. I miss the liaisons with the gay rugby player. I remember him whispering, "Ssh, can't afford to give the neighbours the idea that we're in bed." That's what made it so exciting — the danger of it all. Thank God, Russell has faded, otherwise the two of us would surely be double-trouble for any willing man.

The door is flung open. Deborah stands there, dishcloth in hand and green eyes aflame, nagging, "You want to eat?" Her mouth is curled in mockery, her shoulders stiff with the posture of a woman who hates men.

"What about you? You've eaten?" This is Trevor's last straw of kindness and tolerance.

— She's not cooking for *me*! I say, but I'm losing myself in Trevor's stare as his eyes search for the gentle woman he thinks is there. Believe me, there's more to this than PMT.

But he fails to acknowledge my back-seat presence. Instead, gratefully but resentfully he gives in under Deborah's pressure.

— When it's cooked she'll throw it at you! I warn him again.

— Nankavelle, I'm not as unobservant as you think I am . . .

TREVOR SURVIVES THE ordeal of a family visit, her parents scrutinising every detail of him. They look upon their daughter's catch with healthy respect, yet the expression in Daddy's eyes says it all: "What's a nice boy like you . . .?"

During the course of the visit I surface and look around the room, taking in the new faces. I'm my usual polite but timid self. When Daddy shook Trevor's hand I could see in Deborah's eyes that she was rolling the entire scenario around in her mind: What is this? How the hell do I get out?

I feel empathy for the mother. Her face wears a mask moulded by a lifetime of anxiety. It is clear that Deborah has put both parents through hell, and vice versa. Such tensions in the air only make me more keen to hitchhike back to Christchurch.

FINALLY THE BUBBLE bursts. Deborah suddenly announces that she's taking a two-week holiday down south, to Dunedin. There's a suitcase on the bed and she's piling clothes into it. Trevor is unfazed by the idea of her small break "down South". But what severs the last thread of confidence he has in her is the sight of something being folded carefully and placed in her suitcase.

"Ooh, sexy!" he says. "Didn't know you had a teddy suit."

Deborah closes the lid and stands there silently for a moment. "I've got my period, so you can forget about sex."

"Oh, yeah." The sun is sinking in his eyes. He asks, "So why're you taking the teddy suit to Dunedin?"

She laughs, now avoiding eye contact. "It's nothing. Just want to show it to a friend while there . . . "

"Oh, okay." He doesn't believe her, so he pushes the issue. "A woman friend of yours?" Already he knows the score.

She has a look of grey shame and speaks quietly with a well-needed dose of honesty. "No, Steve's a good friend." And now the lie: "I just want to show him. He'll get a real laugh out of this."

Within a week Trevor has left the rural love-nest that never was. He returns to Christchurch, a gutted fish.

t w e n t y o n e

*I*T'S LOSS THAT I can't stand. Losing somebody is the ultimate of all
pains. It's that moment, as if frozen in time, when a person turns his
or her back and walks away. I'd rather crawl through a pit of fire than
stand there with my heart in my mouth. Loss is not about saying goodbye
— it is a slow, internal death.

I describe loss to Ralph and as he listens I note a wet glimmer in his
eyes. For that brief instant I love him totally — this therapist is human, I
can touch his heart with mine after all! "It feels like an orange," I
explain. "Imagine that the orange is my heart . . ."

Ralph's face is expressionless. His eyes say it all. And inside the abyss
the Mad-Child is asking, Does Ralph love *me?*

I continue describing pain as though I am a teacher outlining an
experiment: "If you take the orange in both hands, squeeze it until the
juice spurts out — well, it's like the blood being crushed out of it."

In a soft warm voice Ralph suggests, "But what you're feeling isn't in
your chest?" It's a statement and a question. He goes on to explain how
the mind can involve feelings which affect the body.

I already know this, and now I'm angry. "In horror movies a wooden
stake is driven through the heart of a vampire. I feel that."

"You mean emotional pain? Physical?"

"Yes! My chest hurts." I'd like to tell him that sometimes when I'm
alone and think about my father, well, the ache is unbearable, the grief
consumes me to where I feel as if I'm dying.

Often in therapy I've told Ralph, "I'm dying!" and then a deep-seated
rage opens up from behind the abyss and Son of Sorrows rants on for
great lengths of time, cursing all men who are fathers.

— Fathers. Fucking bloody fathers!

A BUMPY VAN ride through the Whitford Tip. The stench of rotting refuse
permeates the air and comes through the old rubber sealing around the

passenger side-windows. My parents, brother, and sisters are curiously looking out, but the view is far from pleasant. Muddy brown tyre marks, and the invasive noise of bulldozers shovelling several thousand tonnes of rubbish: old, unwanted home appliances, broken prams, rain-soaked paper Kleensaks, tree trunks, tyres, rotting cardboard and paper, old television tubes.

I'm delighted to see my favourite birds hovering about the mounds of refuse, scavenging for food. Seagulls are much hated by some people, but for me they're symbolic of surviving all forms of abandonment by living off the scraps of society.

Dad eases the old Thames van into an empty area before the huge cast-off pit and by now we kids are piling out to screw up our noses in disgust at the overpowering smell of things decomposing, things dead.

I'm caught up in a fantasy, imagining how many carts I can build with all the broken pram wheels. I'm also in awe of how the seagulls are territorial about their own found portions of stale and rotting food. They lower their beautiful white heads and with open beak and a "U" shape neck, run toward other gulls shrieking, "This is mine! Mine! Mine! Mine!"

These observations and daydreams are shattered a moment later when I'm brought crashing back to earth by the sight of my family, all reseated in the van which is driving away. I panic and run after the van, but it still keeps moving ahead. A great distance is growing between me and the family. I now run faster, waving my arms about and screaming as if I'm being murdered. For these few seconds I am utterly destitute. Like the seagulls I'll have to survive, somehow.

My poor mother and father are taken aback. When the van has been driven in reverse and the side door opened, I clamber into the back seat where I howl my eyes out. Mum is beside herself with apologies. Dad is trying to smooth out the situation by laughing and joking about how they wouldn't forget me. "We made a mistake. Sorry, we couldn't leave you behind."

But I'm a child. How can I begin to comprehend such a genuine but innocent human error? All I can see is their driving away as deserting me. My heart is feeling abandoned. Something so basic, so seemingly trivial, will prove to be a painful trauma in later life.

THE ZOMBIE IS braindead. You can be forgiven for thinking that he's blind. He walks without seeing or hearing. You can't surprise or frighten him — even if you led him into a blazing furnace he wouldn't notice a thing, he'd simply walk through the flames unaffected.

He doesn't have thought processes, is barely conscious, and does absolutely nothing other than amble through life as a dead, empty soul. The Zombie is perpetually dead, because he's never been alive. You'll certainly see him coming, for everywhere he goes people toot their car horns, others abuse him verbally.

His face is expressionless, his breathing silent. His body moves forward — no gait, no mannerisms. There never have been any physical characteristics to make original his lifeless non-personality. He is only walking in one direction — forward, to find his beginning and to enter into the light after his end: through unconscious darkness to warmth, his breath, light and life.

The Zombie remains dead. Let him walk through his resting-in-peace. Hit him, curse him, throw cold water in his face — it doesn't matter, because you can't hurt the dead.

HER NAME IS Janine. Michael and the other neighbourhood kids laugh behind her back. She's no oil painting: fat, freckle-skinned, with carrot orange hair and big saliva-coated teeth.

My eleven-year-old heart is sickened when I hear Michael say about her, sarcastically, "Ah, Raquel Welch. Ooh, she's so beautiful!" I get his meaning: she's ugly, a bore, and who can love somebody like that?

I love Janine. We're in the same zoo, her and me — hideous animals on display, only fit to be teased — other people's entertainment. I long to open up to this sad sixteen-year-old girl. I'd like to tell her that what's inside is more important than the flaws of nature. I think about her often — kindred spirit, that kind of stuff. But what can I say to her? Anyway, I'm not given the chance. Should I resist the peer pressure to laugh at her ugliness, my No-Exit Street friends would surely ostracise me more than ever. I'm lost for words in her presence. My skin prickles and an ache radiates from my gut, up into my chest, because I feel her sadness.

I've visited her house with Tau, been inside that bleak lounge where there's nothing other than an old ruined couch with springs poking through the threadbare cover.

Dear girl. She never complains, never lets on that she knows the other kids are sniggering behind her back: "Big tits. Put a sack over her head before you fuck her." And how Michael and his brothers laugh! I fail to understand how such a tragic creature with her deep, inner beauty can be cheap conversational material over bottles of beer and stolen cigarettes.

I'll never forget seeing Janine sitting in the long weedy grass of an abandoned property, crying her eyes out. That was before I heard through Aunty Rona that Janine's mother died. Poor girl came home from Otahuhu and found her mother dead, cold, on the kitchen floor.

And so we crowd into Janine's lounge, me and a few other two-faced kids. I'm distressed to witness such poverty. A two-storied, run-down Housing Corporation unit with shabby carpet, sheets for curtains and kitchen cupboards so empty even the mice would starve to death. She cries for her mother, and over the course of several weeks, Janine changes. The victim becomes the survivor.

I wish that I could do something. But what? Janine has a job now, at a plastics factory in Carbine Road. She buses in and out of work and I wait hopefully by the bus stop on Travis Road to see her, to appreciate her, to say something, a pat phrase like "You'll get through this, Jan." But I'm not yet wise or educated in the school of life. I'm just somebody who is waiting at the bus stop, feeling her pain. No food, no furniture, not even a social worker on her doorstep to say, "Hey, I can help you." Damn the system of 1979 — the hungry kids roam the streets, empty bellies, vacant eyes saying, "Don't give me all that love shit!"

The truth of the matter is that what I feel I can't express. Janine, you will always be loved and remembered.

PAWPAWS, JUICY, YELLOW, but too high off the ground because the tree top almost reaches the upper level of Janine's house. Tau and I have shaken the hell out of that tree. We've battered the branches with Aunty Rona's broom until several of the luscious, densely seeded fruits fell from the tree. I'm in no doubt that Aunty Rona will lecture us when we get home to Tau's house. She'll be wondering what has happened to her broom, why it isn't in her wash-house. Tau had to crouch on all fours in the end while I stood on his back — yeah, finally the fruits came down.

We eat our pawpaws on the ramp where mossy concrete trails down into murky brown water. No rowing boats on the foreshore today. To slice into the moist fruit centre is an art in itself. The fishing knife is sharp (the same one we used to nick our hands and hold them together, brown skin to white, blood brothers forever!); we scoop out the black seeds and then "go halves", equal amounts shared, acidic juice dribbling down our chins.

The pawpaw tree has often saved our lives — from hunger, when I've been in a foul mood because big brother has been taunting me and kicked me out of the house. "Uh, fuck you! Stick dinner up your arse — I know where there are pawpaws and peaches!" Or feijoas, apples, plums. I'd banged on Aunty Rona's door many a time, asking for my beloved Maori friend, and despite her refusal to let Tau outside I'd waited under the sitting room window for him to jump out and join me.

As best mates Tau and I have a lot in common: we both have older brothers who treat us like shit, we're both full of anger and keen to grow up. Independence doesn't belong to kids like us. Of course, we get our own way in the end by means of escape. We've jumped out a good few windows, called out to one another as prisoners or friends on the outside:

"Hey, Black-balls, you there?"

"Fuck up, Nannygoat. Hine's coming down the hall!" His voice is often tense with anticipation. "Nannygoat? You there?"

"Yeah . . . "

"Got the fish hooks?"

"Course." I'm under the window, smoking a cigarette.

"Hey, you pakeha shit, catch this!" he slings a paper bag in my direction.

Dough? "Eeling!" I'm also prepared for a tide's-out swim.

Our methods of escape are fantastic. Day or night we listen for one another's code. When the moment is right the "prisoner" leaps from the window ledge. I'd once tried, quite foolishly, to attract my friend's attention by hurling small green peaches at his window, only to hear Tau's older sister shout down the hall, "Eh, Mummy, Nannygoat's throwing peaches at Tau's window."

On this occasion I'd moved away from the window and pressed my back up against the house, between two rooms. I was waiting there for the fuss to die down when, a minute or so later, Aunty Rona appeared around the side of the house. "Nannygoat? Whatchoo doing there? Boy, you'd better get inside before I slap your ears!"

By this time Tau had his window wide open and was laughing from the ledge, "Ah, Nannygoat, you got catched!" After his mother ushered me inside the house, she lectured me, "You'd better get your honky arse on that couch . . . you hear me?"

"Yes, Aunty." I was secretly pleased to be "caught" because it meant that Tau and I could spend the evening laughing and joking together.

Aunty Rona knew I'd been arguing with my older brother because her face was both loving and scornful. "You had a feed?"

"No . . ."

Later in the evening, Tau and I would trail off down to the kitchen and watch Rona press out two lily-white rounds of Maori bread. Her chubby face would be serious, her eyes fixed on the flour and water in front of her. I'd marvel to watch the way her soft brown fingers made contact with the dough. It seemed so easy but the wonder of such a skilled tradition would eternally belong to her.

t w e n t y t w o

THERE IS A crackling monologue inside my head. Somebody is quoting poetry I've never heard of. The voice is male, unmistakably old, and whoever he is, I like him. I have no fear, the poet is far from being a threatening existence within.

Words continue to roll through me like waves of green sea water. I listen to the poet's distinctive Scottish brogue as he recites,

> When you have tidied all things for the night,
> And while your thoughts are fading to their sleep,
> You'll pause a moment in the late firelight,
> Too sorrowful to sleep . . .

I usually read poetry only when absolutely necessary. I tend to think of it as compulsory reading for classes studying English language. I can't say that I enjoy hearing it read aloud either. The only poem I can recall, somewhat hazily, from schooldays is *The Ancient Mariner*. I can't remember a single word of it, nor could I tell you what it was about — except that I think there was an albatross in it — but I do know the poem stirred up deep emotions that I would otherwise not have experienced. Perhaps it was the salt in my blood? My family are all keen fishermen, after all. Now I'm comfortable with an old poet giving recitations inside my head, and so I listen:

> . . . The large and gentle furniture has stood
> In sympathetic silence all the day,
> With that old kindness of domestic wood;
> Nevertheless, the haunted room will say,
> Someone must be away . . .

Who is this tenderly spoken old fellow? Have I conjured him up? And, if so, how? Nothing surprises me these days. I'm often discovering new voices inside me, but it pains me greatly to be pushed into a dark recess while they invade my body and mind. Radio station, satellite head? I have to joke, be amused by it all, otherwise if I don't laugh every now and then I'll be sure to find my own crazy face in the mirror.

The old poet speaks in rhythm and rhyme. I don't want to ask who he is or where he came from. That would be dangerous. I'd open my big mouth, and some white-coated bastard would feed me yellow Melleril tablets and confine me to a padded cell.

Been there, done that. I'm not crazy. Really, doctor, I'm not . . . am I? And the old poet finishes the verse,

> You bend your head and wipe away a tear.
> Solitude walks one heavy step more near.

Should I applaud? Too late, he's gone.

THE CHILD'S NAME is Trouble. I learn of her existence by accident.

During one of my non-lazy days I decide to bake a loaf of bread. I have the oven prepared, the yeast is fermented; now all I have to do is clear the bench and wash the dishes. I feel Trouble coming, sense myself shrinking to become her body size. Once she's surfaced fully, her shortness convinces me that she is a child of about nine. She reaches for the teatowel . . .

— How come? How come the hand is hurting? she's saying.

The memory comes to me, and at the same time she is receiving the recall too. I know this by the way she is reacting: she's trying to use the tea towel as a bandage for my hands.

— You got burnt too. She's surprised, and I feel her eyes open wide. Through a dark recess I try to slip behind her face, but my features don't fit. Instead her anxiety filters through to me and the powerful image of a hand pressing onto a piece of cloth. What both of us are seeing is an attempt at arson. But where? Who? I'm asking myself, and sure enough, I receive an answer:

— Fuck, it hurts. Because YOU stopped me, Nankavelle!

It is Son of Sorrows. I feel condemned by his words. So, that is it! Son of Sorrows was in so much pain in that house of my childhood that he wanted to destroy it. Almost succeeded. An act of utter desperation. Revenge for the suffering that our body had to undergo . . .

— In THAT house! he is saying. And now I have compassion for him. My eyes are watering because he has touched my heart — and also because the girl, Trouble, has bent my hand backwards to run cold water down my palm.

— Why a box of matches? I ask Son of Sorrows, not wanting to acknowledge his pain.

— I couldn't stand another fucking day of it! He's reaching for the hot water tap and trying to drag our hand under it. You escaped the pain. You had less on your shoulders. You were loved!

— No, this is 1989, I remind him. That house is gone. I urge him to talk further but Trouble is starting to cry.

— I'm in big trouble, she whimpers, I'm going to be punished now! She's making our face crumple, but at last Son of Sorrows turns away.

— Fucking petrol's in the shed! . . . All at once I understand his fear: eliminate the enemy before the enemy eliminates you. I feel guilty for being a coward, leaving the matches in Son of Sorrows' hand.

— I'm as much to blame.

The girl is wiping our hand with the teatowel. — No more?

No. The pain *will* go. Now I can turn my back on Trouble. I can draw an imaginary line through my head: my half, your half. The girl fades, the bread rises. I eat, think, worry, and then slink off to bed, hating myself for being such an oddity.

— It's all a matter of survival! pipes up someone. Just for the moment, though, I'll ignore that voice and hope it goes away.

Sleep comes just before dawn.

twentythree

YOU DO NOT *need to know my name. I come from a quiet place. Like a vampire I am unable to tolerate daylight; I am accustomed to operating in the dark.*

I sleep by day — not in conjunction with The Body but in my own internal private place. I patrol the house by night. My eyes see very well in the dark and I move swiftly, silently on my feet. My function is superior to those special qualities of the other selves.

I am a night watchman, a protector. I am a living breathing alarm. I can hear footsteps of passers-by, out on the street at night. They are usually drunk people coming home from night-clubs and pubs.

I am unique in the fact that I am able to hear sounds from a considerable distance away. I hear vibrations which the human brain normally filters out. I am also a great detective. I sight danger as it approaches, know who is coming and going in this street, at all hours of the night.

Allow me to tell you about feet. I hear all the footsteps of people passing and I analyse their patterns of walking. An example would be an angry female; she makes quick stepping movements on her feet. Her shoes are no doubt comfortable, probably made of soft material, not leather. This female is wanting to get somewhere fast. She never pauses and her walking is rhythmical. I know she is angry because the urgency of her gait indicates that some deep thinking process is going on — preoccupation of some form.

These alert senses have kept me alive and also allow fearful other selves to give The Body a rest when tired. This house has been divided into zones. There is an escape route should some emergency or danger to other selves occur. I have another escape route which I do not care to mention. You see, I trust nobody.

Placed around the house in various strategic sites are weapons — a wooden baton, carving knife, scissors, and other heavy objects. In the event of an intruder breaking in I would launch myself into defence mode. I am very strong.

As mentioned, I seldom sleep at night but, for want of rest, I switch off communication to other selves. I rest from my own thoughts, too, by dreaming without sleep. I am able to dream and remain alert simultaneously. I escape to other locations which are self-created via the power of imagination — I call this "meditation".

I carry out these processes while The Body is standing and without movement. This is solely to recharge the Mind and Body each of us share. During this rest I am still able to hear a leaf blowing about in the gutter, keys in a car door, and other nocturnal vibrations which continue to intrigue me.

While patrolling the house by night, room by room, I am slow in movement, so quiet on my feet that I cannot hear my own footsteps. I must be efficient, conserve energy, should I need to fight off an intruder.

I scan every facet of the house and see very well in darkness. I look and listen for anything unfamiliar: shadows — yes, shadows do exist in a darkened room, set off by moonlight, digital clocks or freezer lights — a breeze, rattling noises. Any change in air temperature warrants an investigation.

I write in the dark. This is done by feeling the edges of a piece of paper — my fingers search for a ridge where the paper ends. I visualise these measurements, transferring size calculations from my mind to pen motions on paper. Smaller size paper will involve small hand movements, gripping the pen tightly and pressing the arch of my outer palm onto the page. Writing on larger paper involves looser, fluid motion of my fingers and wrist. The right side of my cupped palm and little finger must be kept on the page. I write in the dark because I like to leave messages for other selves to read in the morning: YOU ARE SAFE WITH ME.

I roll cigarettes in the dark. Once again, sound is a good indication of where a rice paper begins and ends. I make coffee in the dark and, as yet, I haven't accidentally electrocuted The Body while plugging in the electric jug.

Though I am able to see in the dark, some rooms have lesser degrees of light and shadow than others. What differs are the finer details in appliances and furniture which are often distorted or missing. Many objects are mere outlines.

I can measure shape and size via visual observation but I could not play a deck of cards, for example. Sensory observation and familiarity with my surroundings are why I can function in the darkness.

My nights are seldom boring. I am becoming less afraid of a possible confrontation with an intruder. I fear that one day I may kill some foolish burglar whose only goal is to steal in the quiet of night.

Nightwatching has always been my life. I must protect all the others, includ-

ing myself. The Body may walk around with me in it but the other selves sleep peacefully, knowing that I am their passport to safety and security.

Actually, I am afraid of the dark and this is why I will not succumb to it and rest. A resting body, lying asleep on a bed, is utterly vulnerable. Then again, perhaps darkness itself is not frightening: what comes out under the cover of the dark, or the possibility of it, scares me.

I will never allow Our Body to come to any harm. The Others call me "Night Eyes" but this is not my name.

I COME OUT of this thin smoky fog to realise that I'm standing at the dining table by the lounge windows. In my hand is an A4 sheet of paper. I look at this leaflet on which a map of this flat has been sketched in pencil. The top of the page reads: ESCAPE ZONES. Each "Protection Site" has been marked with a cross. It is quite an elaborate plan. Locks on the front and side door have been highlighted with a circle. An extra set of door keys has been ascribed the letter "A" and noted as hanging under the dressing table. The letter "B" is highlighted on all window sites. (Later I check these sites and find sharp tacks along each window sill.) "Patrol Routes" have been marked as a straight run along the hall, looping into the lounge, bathroom, and kitchen, and back along the hall.

I place the map on the dining table, close my eyes for a moment before heading into the kitchen where I fill and boil the jug. I can't be bothered unpacking a tower of boxes which clutter up one corner of the lounge. Instead I recline in an old chair, shut my eyes again and try to relax. During my rest I recall a playful event from childhood:

A gaudy old pink rug lies by the hearth of an ugly, marble spotted fireplace. The after-school dregs of winter sunlight filter through the large paned windows. I'm sitting cross-legged in the centre of the rug. I close my eyes and strain to concentrate. I feel light-headed, almost giddy with happiness and begin my rapid ascent into the world of childhood imagination. Gradually the rug rises off the floor. "Hold on tight!" I shout as a cool wind blows over me. I grit my teeth, feel breathless, as the magic rug wavers, suspended in mid-air, and hovers over the carpet. The rug slips through an open window, gathering speed, gaining height. I glide over the neighbouring houses, shouting, "Hooray!" as I pass over grassy suburban yards. Low billowing clouds with the texture of mashed potato drift by. I watch busy streets and a steady flow of traffic below me. Each car becomes matchbox size, as if I could reach down from the sky and scoop a handful of vehicles up in the palm of my hand.

My carpet ride becomes an exciting experience as I twist and turn, jostle about, left and right on the pink rug. "Hold on tight!" I shout again when the magic carpet circles about in dips and dives to avoid seagulls on a possible collision course. The speed at which I am travelling begins to frighten me. My hair is blown into my face and every muscle in my body is tense. I have no idea of where I am going. The carpet enters the stratosphere. I can no longer see the earth beneath me. About me is a fog and layer upon layer of thick clouds.

I begin to fear that the magic carpet is taking me somewhere I don't want to go.

"Stop! Stop!" I'm shouting. My eyes are dry and gravity has pulled my cheeks back to expose bones. My mouth feels like the inside of a dried apricot with a dry flannel tongue. "Slow down! I want to go home!" but I seem to be hovering in a dimension of whiteness, nothingness. When I can't stand it any more, this fear of having no control over my destiny, the magic carpet takes a dive. I'm spiralling downward. Here come the clouds, here are the houses, roads and cars, getting bigger and bigger. I'm scared that both the carpet and I will smash into the hard earth. As suddenly as this magic ride got out of hand, it's over. I'm home — slam, bang, shattered glass and broken bones. I touch myself to check that I'm still alive. Nothing's really broken, but I'm trembling all over.

Jack and the Beanstalk — I want to go there, an internal voice pleads with urgency. I want to hear the harp sing. I want to climb the beanstalk. Throw away the beans. I want to see the giant . . .

I ignore this new voice. I'm still shaken by the apparent realness of the magic carpet ride. Time and consciousness are lost from this point. Whenever I get the chance and I'm alone in the lounge, I pick tufts of wool out of the old pink rug. I hate that rug, now.

THERE IS AN enormous sensation of pressure building up inside my skull. A headache so intense that the pain becomes intolerable. A crushing sensation fills me. A feeling of impending death. I can scarcely move for fear that some blood vessel will pop. Anxiety? Blood pressure? My vision begins to swirl and I sway on my feet before making an attempt to reach the bed. I can hardly comprehend what follows . . .

My vision range narrows. From full view it constricts until the room around me disappears. I see two tiny circles of light approximately the size of ten cent coins. Oddly enough, to experience this microscopic vista I have to look down two tunnels, each seeming twenty miles long. I may as well be peering down two lengthy hosepipes.

I hold out my hands but to see my arms is a frightening realisation that the hands at the end of these tunnels are an unbelievable twenty miles away. How is this possible?

Now, I won't even endeavour to move. I'll stand still until this unexplainable malady passes. But my heart is pounding, pure terror. The impossible has become possible. The cranial pressure reaches it peak. Partially blind, in fear of this strange phenomenon, I believe there is only one way to make it stop: "Our Father who art in heaven, hallowed be Thy name, Thy kingdom come, Thy will be done on earth as it is in . . ."

I'm screaming but am disconnected from my body. I am nothing but the sound of my own terror and there are three other voices, each with a distinct dialogue coming out of my mouth. I'm shaking from head to foot, crying so forcefully that at brief intervals, between the accusations of others I don't know, my ears become deaf. My screams are internalised like an amplifier thumping inside my skull, sound distorting, then no sound at all.

What words can I use to describe the violent physical struggle that grips my body? Somehow I am in the centre of the tunnels while three others are pushing and shoving me in their battle to entomb me within the abyss. I must fight, for if I don't I'll disappear, and that could mean I may never come back. The others are firing allegations. I try so goddamned hard to remain strong, but warm tears slide down my face.

— Aw, shit. Lemme come out. Aw! Wanna be here too.

— Eh? If you don't mind, I'd quite like to be here too. Nankavelle, darling, you don't exactly cope very well, now do you? Still, you always were an odd child . . .

I'm bursting open with the most profound sensation of black rage oozing out of me. I'm in Shit Street. This is where I'll be taken over by one of the three intruders who've surfaced from the abyss. The third self is Son of Sorrows, the most volatile of all, cunning, manipulative, clever.

— Look in the mirror, Nankavelle. See me! I'm better than you. Not so strong, are you? But then again, you did sell out to the Uncle. Fuck. How does it grab you, Uncle's boy!

— What do you mean? I say, bracing myself for the cruellest fight I'll ever endure.

— Come on. You remember, don't you? Son of Sorrows' presence in the tunnels is larger than life. This is to become a shit-shovelling of truths, memories I don't want to recall. I play ignorant and now he pulls the rug out from under me: a memory from childhood seeping into my mind. He savours my response which is pain and disbelief.

— Go on! Vomit! You did exactly what Uncle wanted you to do. Innocent boy? I think not.

— I don't remember . . .

— Now you do.

I relive the sick moment long ago when the Uncle and I did things. The betrayal of my body. Secrets. I don't want to know!

— Hurts, does it?

— I don't feel it . . .

— Oh, but Nankavelle, you do.

I'm quivering from head to toe. I'm shell-shocked by what I'm recalling, what I am being forced to remember — he's telling it to me, spelling out the deviant event like a sports commentary. I am so utterly close to losing it. Teetering on the edge of a truth that hurts like hell. I have to be strong . . .

— But you are weak.

— Go away! And now I open my mouth and I'm shouting out loud to an empty room. "My God, I can't cope with this!"

— Why are you shouting? You're losing it, Nankavelle, aren't you! Go on, quit, Son of Sorrows prompts me.

"You want me to quit? You all do!"

— Do we? I think you're paranoid. Like the family say — schizophrenic.

— That's a fucking lie! I won't quit! And more tears flow. I must be strong.

— You realise they were right all along, the family. You're their poor crippled, mental little idiot.

This is the breaking point. Three voices are echoing inside me, slandering me, picking away at me and digging up every fault and failure I've ever endured. I hang on in until I'm reduced to a state of emotional ruin. At the stage where I fear I'm about to do something stupid — like run off for a repeat prescription of Stelazine and a pep-talk about how I'm socially disabled and should rest up, go for nice long walks around the river — the tunnels close completely. My normal vision immediately returns and I drag myself across to the bed where I weep with sheer relief that I've survived another bid for take-over. I chainsmoke and wonder if psychology is just a heartless, bullshit profession.

When I yawn and turn down the bedcovers, a message filters through from Fourteen:

— You okay, Matthew?

— I think so.

— What happened?

— Fourteen, hon', I don't know.

— There were others? New others . . .?

— Smart girl.

Softly I cry, the cat smooching about my face. I speak to the cat, "Oh, Colby. I'm so bloody lonely yet I've all these hidden people tramping through my life. You understand, puss?" She nuzzles herself into my armpit and stares up at me, moon-eyed. The cat understands.

— You forgot to feed her today . . . Trevor Daniels gently prompts.

"Oh shit . . ." I crawl out of bed, carrying the cat under one arm, dumping her before her plate while I fossick about the cupboards for Biscats.

twentyfour

A WOMAN'S VOICE prattles away inside me. On and on she lectures me, saying:

— I simply WON'T accept this situation, darling. Of course, you DO hear what I'm saying, don't you? And I WON'T hear any more of that NONSENSE you've been saying. For godsakes, darling, SURELY one can expect better of you — unless there is good reason as to WHY you feel the way you do? Really, Nankavelle, enough IS enough! Is it not time that you moved on from the absurd position you're in? How I hate, simply HATE to upset you, darling — and be assured that I do think admirably of you — but, for heaven's sake, if you're going to explore the reasons why us Others are here, then don't forget that you were the one who originally needed us. And who'll believe that what you say is true? Oh, you CAN be SUCH a trial at times. One can never fathom why you should want us to appear to the world? Aren't you the one who's been hiding from society? Be reasonable, lovey, if WE appeared to that god-awful quack of yours . . . can you be certain we wouldn't end up in THAT place? You KNOW I dislike hospitals . . .

I HAVE A dream: I'm inside a mirror maze weaving my way through convoluted alleys of wall-to-wall silver glass. I'm losing track of what is left and right. I can't look into all the mirrors because I don't like what I see: distortions of myself. I am fat and squat, tall and slim. My face is changing, going through a cruel evolution in which I'm persecuted by other faces:

— What did you expect, Nankavelle? Alice in fucking Wonderland?

I seem like a Frankenstein creation. My face is thin and my eyes are black pools of rage. I look willowy, elegant and very seductive — another woman!

— Hey, she whispers, I put my body on the line for you . . .

A child appears. A girl . . .? Fourteen?

— Leave me alone!

I see many body shapes and sizes. Their emotions are like scars seared onto their faces. Hatred, anger, fear, eloquence, amusement, belittlement, sorrow, bewilderment. I'm running and walking, looking behind me. I hear the sounds of other selves; crying, laughing, teasing, taunting, hoping, praying; hell and heaven.

— Me wanna goes home now! . . . A sad child's plea.

— We hate you!

— I love you.

— It's coming, boy. Got's to run, now . . . A four-year-old boy.

I try to ignore the onslaught of sights and sounds from these mirrored images, all the time weaving my way through the maze, wondering, Who am I? Who am I? And their tormented echoes follow me: Where are we? We can't get out! Knocking and tapping on mirrors, Let me out!

My mind is ovewhelmed by fear and confusion. I'm trying to find my way out of this maze and yet I can't recall any exact point where I entered. I awaken in bed. Thank God, I'm here . . . in my Sherbourne Street flat. I lie here, too afraid to go back to sleep. I fight off sleep for as long as I can.

Sunlight through a high window. Morning has well arrived.

MICHAEL, MY SISTER and I hang about together. We smoke our parents' cigarettes, raid the cupboards, pasting thick globules of golden syrup on bread. We don't care that our parents wonder if we're wagging school or not.

On a long hot summer afternoon we come up with a bright idea to hold a seance. Why not? Ghosts and spiritual issues appeal to our curious minds.

I'm scared. Nicole knows I'm wimping out but I can't ignore the gut feeling inside which says, You're playing with something dangerous! It echoes the warnings of ministers who spout from the Sunday pulpit, "The occult is evil — leave it well alone!" But I choose to push aside their niggling doubts — What makes these adults right anyway? — and, scared as I am, I join Nicole and Michael who are as hesitant as me. It's a risk. Nothing bad will happen.

We gather in the house next door and pull the lounge curtains tight. We light candles and clear off the coffee table. Michael's little brother, Andrew, hovers about the room, his listening ears and wide eyes drinking in every fascinating detail as we talk about the underworld, demons, witches. Won't harm us! Not true anyway?

Enough talk and chainsmoking warms the atmosphere. We all want to see a ghost, watch a dead spirit drag the glass around the Ouija circle of letters. This is a mixture of pure fear and an adrenalin high, like sex, under-age drinking, or my smoking cannabis, while knowing Dad would half-kill Nicole and me if he found out what we were up to. This is much more fun than spin the bottle!

THERE ARE MEMORIES I can no longer shut out. Trouble is, they are fragmented, intermingled with the fiction which is my own perception of the real events that have taken place. Strangely enough, I know what is real and what is nothing more than the angry fabrications of the Mad-Child. I can taste what is real. It is shit in my mouth, shit up my nostrils and in my hands — this is the shit of the 1970s, where I lived in that childhood home, in a street I don't care to remember.

Unlike invented stories, the real memories activate my senses: I can smell the things that offended me as child; I can taste what should never have been put in my mouth; I can also feel the burning itch from bee stings over the years. And what about the well-kept family secrets? My adult body still feels these, even if through another self. I'm eager to tell Ralph that The Mind forgets, but The Body never does.

I don't cope with these memories. I switch into other selves, or the Mad-Child comes out. He wails in darkness, huddled under the bed in my room, knees hugged to his chest, and nobody ever knows, not the neighbours, not my friends, never my family. I find myself doing all sorts of peculiar things, reliving old wounds, tasting a slice of yesteryear once again. Dare I have the courage to say to my family, "I find myself hiding in the closet." For what would they think? Would such an admission allow them not only to eye me with a sideways glance but also to shake their heads and think of that dreaded diagnosis?

Ah, but I do compensate for such painful recall. I'm a writer, a sculptor with words, a disciple of the master storytellers. I also learnt very well, at the age of sixteen in a quiet ward of Sunnyside Hospital, the art of meditation. After relaxing my body I find I am able to create and enter the world of visualisation. It is a place in a realm of its own, man-made, and accessible at any hour of the day or night.

V I S U A L I S E simply means to see with the mind's eye. But psychologists do have it right: Visualise equals Fantasise, equals Escape.

And so . . . I will recreate Jack and the Beanstalk, embroider extra scenic details as I enter up the vine, through the thick clouds and walk toward that magnificent castle. But why should the harp sing? Perhaps the giant will sing instead, "Fe fi fo fum, I smell the scent of my English lover!"

. . . I was swimming in the embracing surf,
with dolphins leading me out to the blue blue current.
And circling motions of the water carried me far away,
to where I splashed with new-found freedom,
amongst a thousand penguins who wore suits of white and grey.
All of us played hide 'n' seek amidst schools of silver fish —
those fish blinked their stark blue eyes, mischievously . . .

I MEDITATE WHEN alone at night. I lie on the bed and play electronic music, trying to paint tranquil seascapes in my imagination. The idea is that by visualising the sea it will wash away any anxiety—-
— I hate the sea.
— Shut up, I say.
— I hate the water!
— Yeah. God, I know, kid. You hate the sand too. And now the Adolescent's memory flows through my mind. I tell myself, This sort of shit is never going to die.
— Yes, it will. The Woman seems confident for a change.

THE WOMAN AND I are communicating now. I gather that her self-esteem is near non-existent and she is as unwilling to trust others as I am. Our dialogues are mostly during the early hours of morning, when others are somewhere in their own spaces within the abyss. The Woman confides small secrets to me, expressing her own concern about the mental state of Son of Sorrows. She claims to be asexual but from the cool edge to her voice I'd say she's been harmed sexually, in what form I have no idea. Her fears and uncertainty about surfacing in The Body are explained to me; she's aware that The Body could be under attack at any time.
— By whom?
— Him. Son of Sorrows.
I question why he should hate The Body so much, enough to destroy it. The Woman tells me Son of Sorrows suffered the most amount of hurts when being abused in the childhood body.

— My childhood? He was there?

— Mmmm . . .

I feel her fear and it causes our shared heart rate to accelerate. I press her for further details but she clams up, saying, Somebody has to protect our body.

— I can't do it. It's not always mine.

— You don't love our body? she asks.

— No, I admit, hating myself for being so cowardly. The truth is, I'm scarcely able to love myself, let alone a body which has become a community facility.

I'm slotting together several more pieces of the jigsaw I've become: the Woman is in her early forties, hates men, is agnostic and is somehow related to my early adolescence. On the occasions when she has surfaced, while I was receding into the abyss, I caught a glimpse of her in the mirror. Her figure is what I'd describe as frumpy, her hair an auburn shade and her breasts full, rounded, heavy. I've felt her warm soft hands clasp the coathanger inside Trevor Daniels' jacket and heard her thoughts: — Why am I trapped? Why must I wear his clothing?

I feel sadness, an empathy for her. She is a woman trapped inside a male body; her feminine physique, which I've seen a reflection of, is all in her mind. Enough so that the reality of it, for her, fooled my eyes.

I've been learning that she came into being when I could no longer cope with the betrayals that were inflicted on my body during the early 1980s. When I couldn't accept a grown man exploiting me, she took over.

I am sorry to think that she fools herself into forgetting one awful fact, that she is not a virgin after all. How remarkable, there is a wounded woman inside me. I regret that I took part in those sexual misadventures, that I had to become Son of Sorrows and others, that she is caught up in this whole deeply complex web.

Dialogue with the other selves is important to me. It is important to all. I keep asking myself, can I take responsibility for reckless events in a childhood which was not entirely my own? I think I should, but the reality of it hurts me to the core.

— We are survivors, an unknown voice often repeats.

t w e n t y f i v e

I CAN'T BELIEVE what he has done! After throwing me into a brief
blackout, Son of Sorrows has had reign over my body and burnt my
hand. I awake to hear his threats, and beside me, scalding water is flowing
out of the hot water cylinder into the bath.

For some time I stand over the basin with my right hand soaking in
cold water. Eventually I drag myself off to bed, the hand throbbing with
near-unbearable pain. I won't be able to leave the flat for several days
now. How can I explain the red swelling to my family?

While thinking about my dilemma, Trevor surfaces.

— You can hide yourself from the world, but you can't deny the others' presence, let alone me!

— I created all of you.

— Yes, except that we are real, Trevor replies.

At this moment I resent him. This is an injustice. All I want is a
reclusive lifestyle. However, Ralph has recently spoken an irritating truth:
"Matthew, you can be introverted . . . but you're extroverted too."

Mmm, I was beginning to loathe my therapist's enlightening observations which cut to the bone.

GOOD OLD THOMAS quotes more poetry, his voice crackling with the
dialect of an aged Scotsman:

> False luve! and hae ye played me this,
> In the summer 'mid the flowers?
> I shall repay ye back again,
> in the winter 'mid the showers . . .

— Thomas? You there? There is no reply. My heart sinks.

— He worries you? It is a childish tone of innocence.

— Yes, Fourteen, he does. He never surfaces into my body.

— He's ancient! I like him.

— So you do, Fourteen. I feel sad, the old poet asks nothing, expects nothing. There's no fight for control, no desire to express himself through The Body. Our body. It's like sharing a haunted house. And me, the ghost?

How can I not feel warmth for Old Thomas? He's just there, a soothing voice amidst the chaos.

WHAT ABOUT THAT new voice? Is it a new self, hiding, waiting for the right moment to slip into my body? This is a comforting voice which lulls me into a relaxed state of mind whenever I'm tense, directing me to inner pathways, making the sun rise above my horizon. I awaken sometimes and pinch myself to be sure that I'm still alive. Ah, I sigh, relief! I'm saying goodbye to an incredible nightmare. They never did exist. Hi, Ralph — God, I had the strangest dream . . .

Who am I kidding? They do exist and I'm dividing, subdividing, spawning new selves all the time. Will it ever stop?

I'm not always afraid. I have to be bold, ask questions, play detective at solving these mysteries — no longer *who* are they, but *where* are they and *why* are they here? But doesn't Ralph tell me I should stop worrying; all will be revealed in time? How much time, though? I don't have a lifetime to waste.

And what would Ralph's answer to that be? "Quit searching and analysing, why, why, why. Communicate with them. Love them."

HI, I'M TREVOR Daniels. *The novel I'm writing here in Sherbourne Street is progressing well. Its title is "Embrace". I often write late, into the early hours of the morning. Nankavelle is aware of my existence — he has been for a long time. What Nankavelle hasn't yet figured out is that there are four of us Daniels selves who all write.*

Nankavelle composes angry, colourful poetry. Caxton Press here in Christchurch turned down his submission of an eighty-page anthology of poetry. A letter arrived several days back now, in which the editor said this type of poetry wasn't what the publishing house was looking for.

He's feeling quite low, sliding in and out of a major depression. I'm hesitant to transmit my thoughts to him. If I did I'd have to be honest and say the poems are cathartic. They read well but are somewhat unusual in structure.

I'm six years older than Nankavelle. My hair is auburn, I have his blue eyes but my hair is long and I sport a well-trimmed beard and moustache.

My novel is not being written alone. I'm tapping into Nankavelle's adolescent memories, which he is mostly unaware that I'm doing. However, he is beginning to wake up to the fact that "Embrace" runs on a parallel with his life. He is linking up with his past now via Ralph's therapeutic expertise. My book is about — in part — his sexual identity crisis as a teenager. To confuse matters, I am bisexual, attracted more to women than men. For Nankavelle the act of making love is a painful, confusing ordeal. Sex is in his mind. His body is at times separated from all physical feeling. That is to say, Nankavelle and I share an equal partnership in sexual matters: he explores it mentally while I operate the body. In other words, he is the master of fantasy and love, the centre of emotions, while on my part, I'm the erect penis, the kissing, the touching, the physical sensations.

Nankavelle is often unaware of my function in his day-to-day living. I protect him — at least, should I say, his body. I wear a long brown tweed coat and black leather shoes everywhere that Nankavelle and I go. My long coat is a security blanket for him, covering The Body he's ashamed of. He can't walk outside the flat without wearing my coat or he feels naked, vulnerable.

I have to admit here that I am able to bypass Nankavelle's hurting childhood. What's more, I am about to fall in love with a woman called Susan, but this love won't last for long. Nankavelle will emerge and walk away from the relationship.

THE BODY SPEAKS:
Hatred is a rod pushing up through the spine. The eyes squint while the hands hide behind the buttocks far from view, fists clenched to deliver a hard blow. Son of Sorrows manoeuvres the head, turning it away, for he cannot allow the hatred in the eyes to be seen. To avoid making eye contact is to avoid killing. But these same eyes, along with the ears and the sixth sense, are on the alert for the potential kick in the guts. All the while Nankavelle is pleading internally, "Keep control of Us." The hatred is so hard to bear that The Body shuts down and The Mind detours from reality with the erasure of all senses. To be hated by Us means to always watch your back; though such emotion is reserved for enemies only.

RALPH IS BUSY peeling an apple. He's already tried to coerce me into eating. I'm rapidly becoming wafer thin. Several months of self-starvation have taken their toll. I lift both hands to the back of my head and roll the hairband off Trevor's ponytail. Trevor's been here. I glance at my feet. Mmm, I'm wearing his shoes.

My therapist talks between mouthfuls of sliced apple. "There's a book I'd like you to read. It'll help you to understand the time you're missing."

"Time?" I gather my thoughts. The knife slicing through Ralph's apple is causing me great anxiety. I take my eyes off the apple. "Oh? Time?" The convenience of confusion.

"Remember, you're in a time warp?"

"Time warp?" Play dumb, Nankavelle.

"Matthew you're caught between the past and the present. Parts of you are fragmented."

I nod my head. "Yes." I'm aware that Son of Sorrows is glancing momentarily at the short, silver knife.

"I'd like you to find a copy of a book by Molly Brown. It's called *The Unfolding Self*. Try the library, or Scorpio Books should have it . . ."

The Unfolding Self? I'm about to fade, but I block this feeling and remain present in Ralph's company.

"Yes, I want you to read the chapter about sub-personalities."

"Sub?"

"That's right. Remember? We've talked about the Killer."

"Oh, yes." This moment of truth is as clear and defined as forked lightning, a focal point to start from. The Killer . . . yes, Son of Sorrows.

Ralph shifts in his chair with a slight bucking of the hips which sends anxious, fearful waves through me. Too late, he's done it. And before I can prevent his surfacing the Mad-Child appears.

— F-f-fuck! Fffuck! F-f-fuuccckkk! . . . His words jar in my mind.

— Go away, you! I try to gain control over the Mad-Child's speech, but instead, I fade into the background, blind but listening to the child's nervous babble.

"Fuck . . . God . . . oh . . . fffuck." He's giggling and flaying his arms about as though he's swiping away a cloud of bees. Next, he assumes full physical posture in my body, hands close to his groin, eyes cast downward, scratching with great agitation at non-existent fleas. A tic tugs spasmodically at the spongy muscle below his eye.

Smiling, Ralph talks very quietly. "Speak to me," he invites, but all the Mad-Child can do is waffle on. Jumbled thoughts tumble out of his mouth.

"Fuck! Oh, f—," he says, and then he's gone, leaving me to face Ralph's music.

"Where did you go? Matthew?"

"I don't know. It's dark inside me but I can hear your voice."

Leaning back in his chair, Ralph is quiet for a moment. I watch him out of the corner of my eye. Is he ignoring me?

— You fuckwit, Nankavelle, don't you get it? He's giving you tit for tat.

— I don't understand.

— You disappear, he disappears. Son of Sorrows is fuming now. You do and he does. Are you blind, Nankavelle? As bloody thick as the Mad-Child?

— Oh, come on, Son of Sorrows. You're paranoid.

— Wait and fucking see then! And I feel his presence withdraw.

"Were you talking to somebody?" enquires Ralph.

"Um . . . No."

It is then that Fourteen puts the therapist's question into perspective.

— Saying something? Yes you were. Ralph knows that you're talking to us . . .

— Eh? Fourteen, he can't read minds!

— He doesn't need to.

As I refocus on Ralph I see that he's pointing one finger to his forehead and tapping it. "You're up here, Matthew," he says. "And too often."

Instantly I get the message. My therapist thinks I'm spending too much time having internal dialogues, blocking out the world around me. "Mmm," I agree.

"Read Molly Brown's book," he insists. His facial expression is deadpan, serious.

My half-hour session is up. As I leave Ralph's office I feel good. Finally I'm beginning to understand who these other selves are and why they're sharing my mind and body.

t w e n t y s i x

I'VE BEEN LIVING here in Sherbourne Street for over five months now. My landlord comes to mow the front lawn on a weekly basis. Every Friday afternoon he knocks on the door and asks how I'm getting along and if the flat needs any maintenance done.

I complain about the hot water cylinder — how frustrating it is to be bathing in only six inches of water. The landlord merely smiles and draws attention to the garden under the lounge window, which is in need of weeding. I panic when he points this out. My heart rate accelerates because I feel guilty. I realise my own laziness and it dawns on me just how high the weeds are.

These days I have no energy. I diagnose myself as being melancholic, when in actual fact I'm feeling very lonely. A Friday afternoon scarcely passes without further complaints from me about the hot water cylinder, which is crudely sited above the bath. What a strange archaic contraption it is. A metal coil protrudes from the bottom of the cylinder. Every five hours a jet of hot steam bubbles and boils out of the system. The bathroom fills with steam, and rivulets of water drip down the apricot walls. I nearly choke, walking past the bath, to get to the toilet during the night. It's like living in a sauna. If I turn the cylinder off, by morning I'll have to bathe in tepid water. Dishes gather in the kitchen sink, rarely done, because there is no hot water. I have the daily choice of having a bath or doing the dishes. The constant boiling of the cylinder keeps me awake each night.

Another oddity about this flat is the twin tub Hoovermatic washing machine. This flat has no laundry area, so once a week I drag the washer out from beside the fridge, bundle clothes and soap powder into it and spend two long hours untangling shirts and pants, which have entwined together during the spin cycle. The dirty water has nowhere to go other than down the kitchen sink. While using the machine, boredom leads to

daydreaming — until I'm wrenched out of idle thoughts because the over-
flow hose has slipped. Soapy grey water spurts out of the flaccid hose and
my kitchen floor is a puddle.

Despite these problems and the poor structural layout of this flat, I am
otherwise comfortable. Nowadays I seldom venture out — aside from a
once-weekly visit to the local shopping mall where I buy essential grocery
items and typing paper. My visits to Ralph have been reduced to a fort-
nightly session of half an hour.

I've made friends with a guy who lives around the corner. He's a short
balding man who pencils kohl eyeliner around his eyes. He's a habitual
reader and appreciates antique furniture. I love the way Stephen has dec-
orated his flat. The walls are adorned with 'thirties postcards; wood-
framed portraits of Victorian women hang above the fireplace. Walking
into his flat is like going back in time. A gorgeous tortoiseshell lamp
glows dimly on top of an ornate study table. A heavy silver cigarette case
glints against the backdrop of a cheerful mid-winter fire.

Stephen and I often spend our nights together. He's a dear friend.
During these late evenings we converse about books we've read and about
issues in the late night television news bulletins. I confess to my friend
that I'm very lonely.

My friend regularly injects himself with homebake heroin. This fascinates
me intensely and I begin to understand what long-term drug addictions are
all about. I watch him pierce a vein in his hand. His blood is drawn back
into the syringe where it mixes with a cloudy substance. It is then shot back
into the vein. When the needle is withdrawn, Stephen closes his eyes, leans
back into a chair and I note that his facial expression is one of absolute
heaven. Moments later his blue eyes roll and flicker. I see white eyeballs
through half-closed lids and as suddenly as this movement has ceased, he
seems brighter, happier.

I'm not perturbed by my friend's liberal drug abuse. He's a registered
addict: legal, above board. In moments of depression Stephen refers to
himself as a "junkie". His is a daily struggle for food and he barely manages to "survive" on the dole. We share meals together, laughing and talking our way into the early hours of morning. We consume coffee as if it
were going out of fashion.

I like to watch my friend apply his make-up, when the sun comes up. I
seat myself on the edge of his bed watching him draw a thin black kohl
line around the edges of each eyelid. Some mornings he brushes deep pur-

ple, blue or orange eye-shadow below each eyebrow. He does this in such expert fashion that I can only marvel at his expertise and choice of colour. He's not a transvestite or transsexual person, but often refers to his facial appearance as being androgynous.

On mornings like these I leave his flat shortly after the sun comes up. I have a short walk around the block to my home. My tired eyes sting and daylight makes me wince. By the time I've slipped a silver key into the side door lock, I'm yawning profusely and nearly swaying on my feet. I walk into my bedroom, take off my clothes and get into bed.

My cat, the black and white Cornish Rex I call Colby, rubs up against me, her white whiskers twitching as she purrs. Her little pink lips pucker at the edges of her black mouth as she gently places her lips to mine. Some hours later I awaken and the day begins at 1 pm.

STEPHEN INTRODUCES ME to a good friend of his. Raymond, aged thirty-four, is an artist and I've heard all about his recent success in getting a ten thousand dollar grant. A gallery in Central Christchurch has put him in a studio-cum-bedsitter and he is to hold an exhibition at the gallery. The down side to this is that Raymond has a problem with alcoholism and poly-drug abuse.

I'm to learn some months later that he has frittered away the grant on alcohol, drugs and easy living. Eventually the gallery will gave him marching orders, his exhibition never getting off the ground.

I don't like Raymond. He's vulgar, a compulsive liar and his everyday speech is littered with lewd sexual innuendo. I feel sick in my gut whenever he turns up at Stephen's door while I'm there.

Foolishly I fell into a trap some months earlier. Stephen and Raymond talked me into posing for a pencil sketch. They suggested that I pose naked but I strongly declined any suggestion of this. Instead I sat there clad in my underwear. For about an hour, late that evening, I sat on a wooden chair — thinking the sketch would show some artistic merit. I laughed and talked with the two of them but still felt embarrassed about being semi-nude. They talked me through it, even helped me to relax, and in my mind I assumed such a portrait would be tastefully created.

I was horrified to be shown the sketch. The so-called "Me" was unrecognisable. A blank paper had been scribbled upon — multi-coloured childish shit. Around a mass of perverse scribble, crude depictions of unloving sex and homosexual activity had been drawn. Finally Raymond added his deeply meaningful interpretation of such a vile creation by embroidering it with words such as FUCK, WANK, ARSE and COCK.

I couldn't believe what I was seeing. I was unsure whether to laugh or cry.

My sense of betrayal was further confirmed when Stephen also gave his intellectual interpretation of what was little more than toilet wall graffiti. He spoke the kind of crap one hears in a gallery where crude art forms are exalted with ridiculous terms like Depth and Meaning. Art? My God, Stephen believes in this shit?

— Nankavelle, you idiot! Leave . . . Go on, fuck off home from these people. Artist? My arse! Son of Sorrows held his breath for a moment and was gone.

My so-called "friends", in their drunken state, went into a further analysis of the sketch. I was so angry and shocked that I muttered a polite, calm "Goodbye" and promptly left. Later, in the early hours of morning, I cried. This had been more than a betrayal on their part. I realised that I'd been used, made a fool of, emotionally abused.

I only visited Stephen a few more times after this incident before deciding to end the friendship.

Rain
Is like pleasure
Is pain and coldness
Is darkness
just like shame

WHEN NIGHT EYES isn't patrolling the flat on these rainy winter evenings, I'm lying awake in bed till late morning hours, eventually falling into the colourful world of sleep. My nightmares are abstract: killers stalking me with carving knives, where I sprint along barren city streets, seeking refuge in shop doorways and other dusty dark places. In these dreams I'm having sex with blond-haired men my own age — except that these men have disfigured bodies, some vomit, others consume my body during moments of great passion where I feel suffocated and sick to the stomach. The colours of these dreams are blood red, violent black sexual rage, and tones of white and yellow light.

In these bizarre REM sequences I'm both saint and sinner. Strange objects weave in and out of each dream: cars without wheels, parachutes failing to open, handsome men with cloven hooves and hairy legs who beckon to me in a foreign language. The themes vary in each new episode: falling rain and autumn leaves crunching under my cold bare feet; I kiss beautiful long-haired women, hold them close to my body, only to realise that they have become unisexual, thrusting their disgustingly large penises at me.

Often I awaken to the sound of my own crying with the overhead light still shining.

"Shit, the light's still on!" I curse aloud, dragging myself out of bed and over to the wall switch which I flick off. I lose myself in the black abyss. Later I can scarcely recall extinguishing the light, and stir again to find the room flooded with brightness. The digital clock reads 5.22 am.

— That's funny, I'm sure that I turned out the light!

— You did. The voice of Fourteen continues, Don't worry, the Woman was up. Reading. She couldn't sleep because a noise outside scared her . . .

— What kind of noise? I'm eager to solve this little mystery.

Fourteen hesitates for a moment. She's afraid of . . .

— What? Tell me, Fourteen.

— The street-cleaning machine. We want to hide when it comes along. When I hear this I'm able to slot another piece into the jigsaw.

— Fourteen?

— Yes? She's nervous.

— When the street cleaner goes past outside and you're both scared . . . Is that why I find myself hiding under the bed?

— Don't know.

— Who are you protecting? Fourteen?

— Are you angry? Her voice trembles slightly.

— Angry? Of course not! I laugh and press her for other details. Who hides under the bed?

— Um? I sense that she's about to disappear into the background.

— You can tell me. The others don't need to know.

— The Boy has to hide too. The street cleaner will take him away . . .

— Who told him that? Come on, Fourteen, you can trust me.

— No, no, she says and withdraws her presence from my body.

I'm left with a fragment of evidence.

— Who's the Boy? I ask myself. The Woman and the Boy are afraid of the street cleaner! Why? Ah, shit. If only I had the answers.

— Snoop! Mister fucking detective!

I try to block Son of Sorrows from surfacing. — Get lost, YOU!

— You'll keep, Nankavelle! He's gone again.

As I turn on to my right side, about to pull the bedcovers up to my neck, I catch sight of a coffee mug on the bedside cabinet. I reach out one hand, extend a forefinger and touch the cup. It's hot!

— Okay all of you, who the hell made the coffee? I hear the Adolescent laughing from a great distance inside my head, as if my inner skull is the size of an auditorium, large enough to hold so many people.

— Not me! He surfaces, smiles, and retreats again into the darkness.

— Things like this really bother me! Why can't you all get out of my head?

— Aw, like it! Like it here in The Body! babbles a new voice I'm becoming familiar with; then it ceases speaking.

— Well, I don't drink white coffee. Ugh, it looks like mud. I pull the duvet up over my ears, and listen to the steady thrum of rain on the corrugated iron roof. Eventually I drift off to sleep. Later that morning when daylight has well arrived, I awake. I feel as if I've been run over by a freight train. Through a haze of white fog I recall fragments of last night's conversation with Fourteen. I check the bedside cabinet to prove to myself that the coffee cup actually exists. Just as I thought. Empty. Who drinks that muck? Halfway across the bedroom I stand on a book. I pick it up. *Anthology of New Zealand Fiction?* The Woman's?

MINI-BLANKS: I'M TALKING into a telephone from inside a phone box — blank — I'm telling Ralph about the difficulty I have sleeping at nights — blank — a cabbage in my hand and a carton of milk in the other — blank — a checkout girl at the local supermarket — blank — walking along Bealey Avenue, the rain falling, wearing dirty wet basketball shoes — blank — blank — blank. Shit, I've lost four days! Where have I been all week?

On a taxi ride I have to ask the driver, "Can you tell me where I'm going?" I place eleven dollars and forty cents into his hand — blank — I wake up at home in bed — blank — Where the hell did that new shirt come from?

Fear. Amnesia. Hell.

twentyseven

M Y SISTER NICOLE lives around the corner from me. We tend to argue if we spend too much time together. We take turns visiting each other's houses, and are both ardent cat lovers. My cat Colby is the sibling to her cat Ewok. Nicole lectures me when she visits the flat: "You're not eating! Are you depressed? You should take better care of yourself. Here, I've brought some groceries. Get your shit together! Eat!"

Every time she says this I groan, and though Nicole holds out in both hands a big bag of groceries, I feel miffed.

"You didn't need to buy groceries. I'm eating," I snap, motioning her to come into the hallway. I don't need to be mothered. Oh, bite your tongue, Kid, she's doing this out of the goodness of her heart.

— Stupid fool, Nankavelle. The mess in here tells the family that you're not coping. As if you ever did cope, you useless shit!

My sister sits down in the lounge.

"Can you drink tea without milk?" The moment I say this I'm acutely aware that I must seem a hopeless case to family members.

— Nankavelle, you *are* fucking hopeless!

I'm standing in the open doorway of the lounge, analysing the expression on Nicole's face. She's both irritated and alarmed. "I'll give you a dollar for milk! What do you spend your benefit on?"

"I don't want a dollar for milk! I can drink tea without it."

"You've got a benefit. You're wasting money and not feeding yourself. I don't want you to starve!"

Yeah, right. And end up in a mental hospital . . . "Go and take your pills . . . You're getting psychotic again . . ." Snapping out of my thoughts, I return my attention to Nicole and give an embarrassed walk-on-eggshells reply. "I don't need groceries. I'm okay. Really."

I'm writing, for godsakes. Who wouldn't be depressed after getting a rejection slip for their book of poetry? Not coping? Maybe. But I can look after myself. It's my life.

Nicole purses her lips. I sense that she's brooding. I feel awkward, pushed into a corner. Groceries, yeah, but what am I? Beggar? Refugee? Charity case? I stand my ground over the issue of milk. My sister turns down the offer of sweet black tea. She's awfully quiet and I feel guilt and anger. Why be ashamed of yourself, Kid?

I chainsmoke as the conversation with Nicole wanes. Some minutes later she kisses me goodbye at the front door. I sigh, feeling ashamed as she ambles off down Sherbourne Street.

— Fuck it, Nankavelle! She's *mothering* you. Be independent!

— Go away, Son of Sorrows.

SUSAN IS A good friend of Nicole's and I've only just met her. I've been here in my Sherbourne Street flat for seven months now. Several evenings during the week I stroll around the block to visit Susan. She likes me. I like her and, of recent times, Trevor's been seeing a lot of her.

"I'm a Jehovah's Witness," she says one day, chubby-faced with hazel eyes glinting.

"Okay . . . " I'm groping for words while a debate goes on between my other selves. It's like a party line of different responses and opinions to Susan's disclosure. Jehovah's Witness. Oh, God, what are you getting into, Trevor?

— God's loves me, too! The little boy's plaintive cry.

— I want to go home now. Fourteen's voice is flecked with sharp tones of uncertainty.

— Ha, ha. God, God . . . love her, you do. Ha, ha!

— Piss off, Mad-Child. Idiot face.

— Was that really necessary? I'm pointing an accusing finger at Son of Sorrows.

— I want Susan, but you want a man! You'll never change, Nankavelle, Trevor is saying.

Tonight Susan greets me at the front door. We hug and kiss lovingly. Trevor is smitten, dreamy eyes, plagued with sexual fantasies. She loves me.

"And do you love her?" Ralph said during a recent session where Trevor sat gooey-eyed in my chair by the window, telling Ralph what he was feeling. The therapist smiled. "Enjoy the feelings. Explore your sexual passions."

146 /

"Yeah," I laughed, my face flushed. But how can I desire men when Trevor loves Susan?

— Poor confused fool!

— Piss off! I transmitted the thought back to Son of Sorrows and felt him knot up with anxiety inside me. This is the first time I've really stood up against his vicious strength. More backbone is what is needed. My war with him has just begun. I'll win out.

Susan prepares cholesterol-free meals. She runs baths. She holds me. She goes on loving me when in actual fact Trevor Daniels is her knight in shining armour. A husband, a father to her young daughter, and a nine-to-five breadwinner is what she wants. If only she realised that all the lives that are "me" are heading in different directions: novelist, comedian, actor, poet, dreamer; homosexual, straight New Zealand male of the true blue stereotype, bisexual; slave to religion and fundamentalist morality; virgin, whore. Our list of personal attributes is already a mile long.

When at home in my flat I find the truth about my face, how traitorous it can be: jealous eyes of the Woman in her shyness and pain, or the cow-brown eyes of . . .

— Fourteen? Is that you?

— Yes.

— My God, you're in the mirror.

— So the fuck am I! Son of Sorrows is there, his reflection peering out at me. Don't I just hate you, Nankavelle. His sarcasm like lead bullets.

I stand my ground against his intimidation, except that I can barely see myself in the bathroom mirror. With Son of Sorrows surfacing in our body I am behind him, overshadowed by his gloom. — I created you, you're mine!, I challenge him. — I can create and uncreate.

His retaliation is cruel. The unbearable pain of hot water on my hand again.

— You sadistic bastard, I groan.

— Be careful, Nankavelle. Just remember, I have The Body too.

THE WALLET IS in my pocket. Trevor is wearing his long coat, and then — blank — nothing. I find myself in a telephone box outside a busy shopping mall, telephone receiver in my hand.

"Are you there?"

"Yes, I think so . . ." I'm shaking with fear. Who is the woman on the line?

"You okay, lovey?" A compassionate stranger whose voice is filled with concern.

"I don't know. Who am I speaking to?" I begin to cry.

"Ooh, lovey, you are in a right state. My name's Jean . . . I think you've dialled the wrong number."

"Where am I?" I ask her, when really, I'm asking myself.

"I can't answer that, lovey. Gosh, you are in a bad way. Can you tell me your name?"

My name? My name! "I don't know. My name . . . uh, I'm sorry."

"It's okay, lovey, you're just a bit confused." She pauses a moment, and crackle runs through the line. "Tell you what. Can you look around you and describe where you are?"

"Yes." I sniff back the tears, my nose stinging. "A road . . . a carpark behind me. There's an intersection in front of the supermarket across the road . . ."

"Are there any street signs, lovey?"

As I peer through the dirty glass the words "telephone card" come into my mind. My thoughts are jumbled but I recall a sequence of numbers, and tell the woman.

"Is that a bank account number? Come on, lovey, don't cry. You'll be alright soon."

"I was dialling the number . . ." A bank? Account number? I don't know.

"Listen to me. You're going to be alright," reassures the voice. I wish I could believe this woman. "You've called me by accident, but I'm glad you did. Do you live nearby? Sounds like you're in a phone box . . . "

"Live? I don't know where I live." All the while I'm looking around me. Nothing is familiar. Zilch. Then a gradual series of revelations unfold, the familarity of possessions. Colby . . . my cat? Typewriter? Ranunculus in the garden? A name enters my head. Ralph? Ralph? Is it my name? My name!

"Tell you what," the kind woman continues, "Mmm, no . . . it's best you stay on the line." She inhales deeply.

"Bits are coming to me now . . ." I'm grasping at barely visible threads of reality, and remember that I have other names. "So, who dialled this number?" I ask myself aloud.

"You there?" the woman is enquiring through the receiver.

She must think I'm a nutcase. My names, what are they?

Confusion deepens once again because another voice, unlike my own, speaks within me. A guide offering directions:

— Walk straight down there. Turn right at the light. Keep on going till you get to number 115.

— Eh?

— Turn there, at that corner. Number 115. Focus. One, one, five . . . Trust me!

Dazed, I turn back to the receiver — blank — I'm gone.

I'M SUDDENLY CONSCIOUS of standing in front of a St Albans weatherboard house.

— Why am I here?

No reply comes from within. I feel eerie because peace, silence, and bliss have been missing for a very long time now. Tears fill the corners of my eyes — the frustration of having a mind which is full of black holes and abstractness. Life is some form of vortex.

— I'm sure that I know the man who lives there . . .

That voice, as soothing as medicine, speaks:

— *You* live here!

— Me? The voice inside my head must be telling lies.

— Look at that window . . .

The image of a large wooden desk comes to me, and a black cat sleeping on a chair under the sash windows. Colby! I've got a cat called . . .

— Think clearly. Don't be afraid.

— Oh, my God! Images of the inside of this house come to me in rapid succession: my large bedroom, the lounge with its gaudy floral carpet, the leaking tap over the sink. Do I live here? The fog is thinning. Within a short time I'm hesitantly edging up the side path. I live here? Blank. I'm erased; stored elsewhere for just a moment. I snap to, once again, with the front door closed behind me, the keys in one hand.

— Trevor Daniels?

Bit by bit, it's all coming back to me.

STARLIGHT PLAYERS, A local theatre company, are running a season of *Pinocchio* at the Repertory. A friend of my mother's telephoned recently asking if I'd be interested in making refreshments for the crew. After giving this a great deal of thought, I contact Leslie some days later. "Yes, okay, I'll do it." A hint of anticipation in my voice.

Later the same week I meet up with her and members of Starlight Players. Dress rehearsals are in progress, so I sit beside Leslie at the back of the theatre to view the activity on the brightly coloured stage. I'm very impressed with what I see, and nervous, too — I often feel inadequate when around bubbly, charismatic people.

The director stands in front of the stage, waving her hands and telling child actors to raise their voices. I feel a great empathy for Pinocchio. Imagine creating a puppet who wants to come alive! Hand-carved face, wooden body, but wanting a fleshy, human heart. Trapped in timber and so keen to become a *real* boy. Enter the wolf. He's cruel, greedy, all teeth and hostility — Son of Sorrows? — and poor old Gepetto, eccentric creator of puppets — old Thomas the Poet? Shitsakes, why am I drawing parallels to my own life . . . ?

Here I am now in a long narrow kitchen, several days later. Through the wall I hear the laughter of children, a massive audience, booing and clapping their hands. I glance at my watch: Almost time. Shit. Make and pour five pots of tea — thirty cups — and coffee as well.

The door opens and I'm instantly beseiged by hordes of people: stage crew, sound technicians, the props and lighting team, and a lot of the cast of vividly dressed child actors. Orange juice! Oh God, Pinocchio and the wolf want juice. The stress of the moment is near unbearable.

— Octopus! You need eight arms and legs.

— Shut up, kid. Oh God, the Adolescent will never forgive me. An idea comes to mind. — Hey, Fourteen, are you there?

— Yes.

— Thank God. Help me, please! Can you pour the orange juice?

— Okay! she beams.

More people are squeezing through the back-stage door. The walls are going to burst! I shift into automatic-pilot mode. Twenty or more actors and crew are politely demanding, "No milk, please!" . . . "Sugar. Two!" . . . "Where's the coffee?" . . . "Orange juice? Where is it?" . . . "Water will do!" . . . "You look stressed, dear" . . . "Oh, so you're the new tea lady!" . . . "Is my tail straight?"

Through a dense white fog I hear myself saying, "Just love your hat!" and "Black coffee? Who wanted black coffee? . . . Yes, I'll collect them later from your dressing room . . . Sorry? My name? Ah? Excuse me. So busy I've forgotten my name . . ." Laughter. Panic. Anger. Fear.

— Where am I? What am I doing?

— Relax, you'll survive this. A calm, loving voice as soothing as a warm bath, liquid smooth like melting chocolate.

— Who are you?

— Don't worry, Matthew. I'm here to help you . . .

Emerging from the fog now, I fully recover my senses. The kitchen is empty and the two stainless steel benchtops are cluttered with plastic cups. Through the door I can hear somebody singing and all the children in the audience are clapping their hands. Pinocchio is doing his number.

— Are you okay now?

— Yes, thanks, Fourteen.

My next ordeal is to venture back-stage to collect the cups that were taken to the dressing rooms. I climb four wooden stairs and enter a world of darkness. The props crew are waiting and beyond, at the edge of the stage, a heavy red velvet curtain is suspended. Beyond that, the child audience. Panic festers inside my stomach. I can't do it!

— No one can see us, Fourteen tries to reassure me.

— No, I can't. I feel sick. Turning my back on the props crew, I walk downstairs into the kitchen. One more round of tea and refreshments? I can't do it.

— You'll be fine. It is that unknown, soothing voice flowing through me again. Strangely enough, for a brief moment I am caught up in a sensation of absolute peace. After that, I black out.

I RECKON A *Good Kiwi Bloke* like me deserves a fair chance to be heard. I don't wanna rake over the shit or anything like that. Jeez, the kid who owns this body is a real complex bugger, eh? I kinda like Nankavelle — wouldn't exactly call him a mate, but he's alright. Got his problems, hasn't he? He gets real worried about sharing his life with us, but I reckon once he accepts our presence, you know, the rest of his life will be a piece of piss, eh.

Wouldn't say I was soft or anything but I get the warm fuzzies now and then. Nankavelle needs to relax — the shrink keeps telling him to go with his fear. I reckon the kid's afraid of losing his life — yeah, but we're not all like that Son of Sorrows. And we're not here by choice. We gotta help Nankavelle out but he thinks we're all the result of his craziness or something. That shrink Ralph keeps saying to him, "You're not crazy!" I don't think the kid understands though. All he sees are those shitty pink rooms and white coats.

Jeez, those hospital shrinks have got a lot to answer for. They're the ones who made Nankavelle crook. Since they dished out that bullshit diagnosis the kid's stopped living — afraid that people think he's loony or something. We try to perk up Nankavelle's spirits but it's like he's died, or about to. I know what's wrong with him: simple, mate, he's confused. The hospital says he's mad, the family reckon he's a pushover and Nankavelle's determined to express himself with all that arty-farty stuff. He writes short stories and letters, and the silly shit rips them up. We hear him telling himself, "I can't do it!" He even yelled at the shrink one day — reckoned it's wrong to be artistic. "Bullshit," the shrink said to that . . . I reckon, no shit, that this shrink wants the kid to let his creative stuff come out. Trouble is, Nankavelle's realised some of the others have talents they want to express too. Must admit, I find writing and music a bit toffee-nosed. Maybe all the kid needs is confidence? Ah, shit, what'm I pissing on about? The kid's spinning out more than ever lately. Love the kid but it's him who wants to end it, so let him go into the dark place, then us others can come out more.

Nankavelle's only just discovered me a few months ago. I was at a party. Everyone was pissed off because I spoke what was on my mind, told them I reckoned feminism is chauvinism in reverse. I also said that a bloke should have a say about abortions, too. The women weren't too keen on me after that. I like women with small tits. And who gives a shit about hooter size?

That poor kid, he nearly flipped out when he woke up in the pub. I went there in the morning and played eye-games with the barmaid. Got a stiff cock just look-ing at her. I went and sat by the window and then the kid had his own eyes again. He looked at my beer and said to himself, "Oh, God, what's happening?"

"Piece of piss, mate," I said. "I've been here a couple of times lately!" Even introduced myself, said my name was Henry.

The kid folded his arms and went real silent. At the shrink's later on he went on and on about how he hated beer. Wasn't his bloody beer anyway! Jeez, that kid's a walking time bomb. Tries to shut out life around him. Reckon he'll fade until there's nothing left of him. Bugger those shrinks — ruin people's lives with their long fart-arsed words.

Things'll change. Nankavelle might accept me, but he chucks his guts when-ever I feed The Body beer. I tell him, "Fuck you, mate. You gotta live!"

If those Others got hitched up or had families, how would the writing ever get done? The writing's been around for ages; goes back to Nankavelle's child-hood.

AFTER THE SECOND matinee I telephone the director and tell her that I can't cope with work at the theatre. She is unmoved but I sense her disappointment. "Sorry," I say before hanging up. I also call Mum's friend Leslie, to let her know that I won't be "tea lady" again. She, too, is disappointed. How can I make her understand my situation? I can't handle so many bright, bubbly people all at once.

"Leslie, I tried. Sorry." Again I hang up, mentally flagellating myself for being such a wimp.

CAMEO FACES At the door
Some disappearing,
And who's appearing now?
Star
Glitter wardrobe
Tinsel lights . . .
Break a leg!

twentyeight

A T THE DOOR I'm greeted with a hug. Ralph asks, "How's it going?"

"Fine." My reply is lifeless, monotone, and I gravitate towards my usual brown chair beside the window.

"Fine?" my therapist queries. "You seem depressed."

"Do I?"

He sighs quietly and scratches his ginger beard. "If you don't want to talk, well, fine — we can always terminate this session . . . You can go home and . . ."

". . . go crazy." My face screws up and I add sarcastically, "I knew you'd say that!"

"Well, as I've told you, there are two choices. You can be a madman if you want to, and end up in Sunnyside. Or we can talk about what you're feeling."

"You have all the answers, don't you!" I'm both angry and amused. I have a need to be childish now. "I might kill myself."

At these words, Ralph tunes out. He ignores me for what seems like an eternity, almost as if I'm not present in his office, a ghost, invisible to him. This makes me hopping mad. Finally he speaks, "Go ahead, kill yourself. There's a busy street right outside this office. But don't expect me to scrape you off the road . . ."

"You fucking arsehole!" Son of Sorrows has surfaced, cursing. "You're like all the other doctors."

Ralph seems unfazed, typically composed. "Tell me what you're feeling," he prompts. "Come on, *talk*!"

The words bite into the warm atmosphere of Ralph's comfortable office. "I hate all men. You should all die — you filthy bastards."

"Why? Because you gave your penis away in childhood?" Ralph's question is at the cutting edge, perfect bait for Son of Sorrows.

"Try living without a cock. But then again . . ."

"You're really angry, aren't you?"

"Angry!" Son of Sorrows laughs coldly, his eyes narrowing as the molten rage pours out of his mouth. "I'm not a *complete* man. I'm cockless!"

"You can change that . . . "

"Can I? But then I'd be like all other men."

"No," Ralph disagrees, "I'm not your uncle. This is Ralph, your therapist, remember?"

"What's the fucking difference? You're all the same." Without a second's notice he's gone. My hands are shaking and I've overheard the conversation between the two of them. I'm jittery as I look about, taking in the familiar surroundings. "I'm still here."

"What do you mean?" It's a straightforward question as Ralph intends it to be.

— Shut your mouth! Don't speak, Nankavelle. He wants you to admit that there are others in here . . .

— But Ralph already knows about Us. Maybe he knows of others too? Trevor is speaking a truth.

— I'll kill you, Nankavelle. Don't you dare fuckin' tell!

Again I black out and the Mad-Child takes over. He squirms about in his seat, the child in disgrace. Ralph offers him a lolly from a glass jar.

— Jellybeans! "No . . . thank you," laughs the Mad-Child as he recollects something distasteful from childhood. He shakes his head from side to side and makes inappropriate body movements. His mannerisms are fragmented, jumpy. A tic appears on one side of his face. In his perpetual state of fear, he tries desperately to communicate with Ralph. The Mad-Child stares down at his shoes, wondering why he's been offered a lolly. In the bizarre framework of his mind, thoughts are jamming and unintelligible nonsense burbles out of his mouth. He covers his body by wrapping both arms around himself. There is a burning pain in his face. "Hit . . . on."

"You want a lolly? I'm not going to hurt you." Ralph's eyes cloud momentarily.

The Mad-Child thrashes both arms about.

— Tomorrow . . . It's coming! Coming! Black police car . . . He stands up and leaves his chair to walk about the office, eyeing the territory. Fear consumes him. He must stand in the corner. It would be dangerous to sit down. He needs an exit, and rubs at the side of his face.

Ralph lowers his voice. "You don't want to sit down?"

"Um, um," the Mad-Child grunts. "Ah, ah . . . going?" He hovers about Ralph's large rimu desk. Can hide under?

"Talk to me?"

The Mad-Child retreats to the abyss. I've now surfaced with minimal recall of the Mad-Child's presence. Sitting down, I say with a bemused smile, "Ralph, I'm still losing segments of time. I've been away but I can't explain how . . . "

"Sometimes, Matthew, you can be a *real* idiot."

"I know," I agree, not catching onto Ralph's deliberate ambiguity, but all of this confuses me.

"Have you got hold of that book yet? The one I've been telling you to read — *The Unfolding Self* by Molly Brown, on sub-personalities?"

"Huh?" How hard it is to fake ignorance now.

— You fool, Nankavelle. Deny the others. Why should we trust this man?

— But Son of Sorrows, I don't know all of the Others.

— Ah, shit . . . You will soon . . .

Suddenly I find myself walking out of Ralph's office. I leave the building feeling perplexed. How can I recall the blanks while in there? The unknown voice, the one which speaks softly with such warmth, informs me as I cross the lights on the corner of Bealey Avenue, — You are lapsing in and out of time, like Ralph said. You're in a time warp, of sorts.

— I don't recall him saying that.

— Don't worry, I'm here to help you. I can erase moments from our life. I'm angry now.

— Bugger off! I can't cope with all this. I'll close my eyes and you'll be gone, all of you!

— Matthew, please, trust me, the voice implores.

As I hurry along the footpath anger is eating a hole in my soul, like acid.

THE BODY SPEAKS:
Fear is like a centipede crawling up the spine. The black spheres of our pupils dilate to larger than usual size. Leg, arm and trunk muscles stiffen as the hairs on the back of our neck bristle. On the right side of the face our lips and eyes spasm; a nervous twitch to show the world that "It" as a self still exists. Our hands tremble and the children are clumsy, knocking over half-empty coffee mugs while the Mad-Child, as if blinded, crashes into closed doors throughout

the house. Fear is the ache of our stomach, the tangled repetition of Stutter-Mouth's words. We want to run. We want to hide. Son of Sorrows defensively prepares himself — "Kill, kill, kill!" — because we are afraid.

FEELING ON TOP of the world, I venture out with the help of Fourteen. A visit to the local hardware shop. While there I rat through the garden and hardware sections to buy a mixture of flower seeds. I then dash home to the flat, put on an old T-shirt and jeans and clear the front garden, piling up weeds beside the path as I go. The seeds are sown.

Eagerly, each day over the following week, I check the garden for signs of life. After several weeks I'm proud to see fleshy green shoots of ranunculus, anemone and poppy sprouting up through the rich soil.

— What a strange time to grow flowers, coos Trevor Daniels. He's feeling in good spirits too and is writing daily his novel about the teenager with a sexual identity crisis.

— Listen here, Trevor, the bulbs are lovingly planted. They'll survive.

— Too right they will . . . and he's gone.

Fourteen tucks a Chocolate Flake bar under my pillow. I find it later in the evening and as I'm peeling back the yellow wrapper she surfaces in my body.

— You'll need that. Trevor's late night writing is draining The Body.

— My body, I say.

— Our Body, she giggles, taking the first bite out of the chocolate.

twenty nine

THE FUCKIN' TROUBLE *in my life, bitch, is livin' in this body of his, eh. To think a special chick like me has to be trapped under all his muscle — and yeah, ah shit, so fuckin' what if I'm a bitch? 'Magine being stuck inside his hairy chest with all those fuckin' male parts. Still. I always thought I should'a bin born with a cock, eh.*

What's wrong with being a dyke, anyway? Women outside of his body are stupid, think they're seeing a brick-shithouse of a man when the silly molls are seeing me! Can't have the sex, though, can I? I'm just a lezzie bound within this body — you fuckin' know — cock 'n all that.

The name's Cody, but Jesus, I'm no watery-eyed, limp-wristed female. Should'a bin born a man, eh! Tell you what, used his lips a few times: may'a bin his mouth but I kissed some'a the pretty bitches he's bin out with. May not be in charge of his cock but I have my fun too, eh. One time, he was with his girlfriend (perfume, small tits, and all that other stuff), yeah, and fuck, I started to kiss her myself and he was real pissed with anger. Made my voice come outta his mouth, eh. Said to this girl of his, in my husky way of speaking, "Hey, fuck, lady — whadda you like about other women?"

Poor girl, she looked at him real strange. Shocked him by saying she'd often thought about being with another woman. Well, shit, he was spittin' alright. Ordered me to get outta his body (His fuckin' body! Who needs a stiff cock, anyway!). He was so pissed with me being fresh on his girl. Said to himself, Is it possible to have a lezzie inside me? Fuckin' sure as hell, I put him right. "Name's Cody," I sez. "Yeah, so I'm a lezzo bitch. So what!" You should'a seen what went on next. His face went like thunder and he stopped doing what the girlfriend was liking. Went sulky and quiet until she asked what was wrong. I killed their moment, eh. What woman needs a man anyway? Men. They're all the same — all meat and no brains. They think with their cocks, raise their fists and ask questions later.

I got up his nose a lot after that night. Started speaking through his mouth, letting him see my desires for women. Really caused a stir, eh! I call a spade a fuckin' spade. Cody's not some feeble-minded bitch needing a man inside (you know what I mean). Shit no, this bitch is a women's woman. Men can go fuck themselves!

This body's nothin' more than a vehicle for me. I gotta make the most'a what I got. I've bin here a long time. I go way back . . . far as 1979.

MY SISTER NICOLE is fifteen now. She's sitting in the gutter at No-Exit Street. Her knees are pulled up to her chin. Her long blonde hair rests on folded arms and she's crying. Under the light of an overhead streetlamp Nicole is fraught with emotion — the kind of tears that come from a girl who is underloved and overburdened.

I sit down beside her. My heart aches to hear her long drawn-out sobs. She's a young woman who has the world on her shoulders. I identify with her pain. In my father's eyes she wears a label and is battered with a constant stream of verbal abuse: she's "the bad girl", whom our father treats as a punchbag. Oh God, if I had the courage to kill him. If I wasn't such a screwed-up thirteen year old, I'd have the guts to complain to a welfare agent or a doctor, to say, "We're cold, we're hungry, our parents have abandoned us."

Nicole and I are of like mind, both having served apprenticeships in victimisation, curses, insults. Our father is living with a new woman. Our mother has moved to Christchurch. Peter, our brother, resents Nicole's presence and mine. He has a girlfriend and baby to feed. There is a vacuum of guilt which empties me out — my brother shouldn't have to feed us, he has responsibilities of his own. I'm ashamed because my being here and my basic living needs intrude upon his life. Poor guy, he makes an immature attempt at filling the role of father.

Nicole has bruises on her body. Dad shouts at Nicole, he drags her to her room. When he shuts the door and I hear slaps, something inside me chips away. At these moments, child though I am, I lose all traces of innocence. To hear the violence coming through my sister's closed door profoundly changes me. I am not a nice person during these moments. I think of committing murder. My hands long to open the cutlery drawer. I want to kill my father because he breaks Nicole's heart and that, in turn, breaks mine. Am I a coward to think of the consequences of murder and change my mind? Childish fool! — too chicken to take that knife into my hands, to raise it and plunge it in.

And here are Nicole and I sitting together in the gutter, puffing on a cigarette. I want to go where she goes — she wants to go where I go — and despite all the sibling rivalry, we'll go where there's food and attention.

We wander the streets, sometimes together, other times alone. Parties, teenagers and booze. My mother would die if she could see us now, but then again, she's in love with a new man and, sadly, she's presumed we kids can fend for ourselves. We do survive. I may be a child but I'm versatile, adaptive. One blow job means several cigarettes, one hand job equals bed for the night.

When returning home from my sexual exploits, I notice that Nicole often cries, for herself, for me. She runs away from home and falls into deep depressions. What hurts so much is that nobody seems to care. Perhaps we've escaped the much-threatened "welfare homes for bad kids", but what's worse? And what about our parents who've escaped legal prosecution?

"DAD NEVER CARED, Ralph."

"In what sense?" he asks, reclining back in his chair, hands folded neatly together, waiting for my reply.

"I don't think he ever loved me . . ."

Ralph interrupts, "Do you think he loves you now?"

The Adolescent suddenly appears. A wide grin spreads across our face and I'm annoyed at being pushed aside. Nevertheless, I listen in on the Adolescent's conversation with my therapist.

"Aw, who cares!" he smirks and transmits a thought to me: Check this guy out. Whaddaya come here for anyway?

The Adolescent starts to laugh. I'm also aware that Speed is grinning through the Adolescent's face though he hasn't surfaced fully. A borrowed mouth, a slice of time — mine!

"The father . . . I mean, my father . . . never bothered spending time with me. Aw, he was always doing everything with Peter . . ."

"Your brother?" Ralph takes his glasses off and proceeds to polish them with a handkerchief.

Polishing glasses: an instant recipe for inner turmoil.

— Grandad! shrieks Speed who recoils within himself with much anxiety. In a second he and Adolescent have gone. I'm left with their memory. I feel rage, thunder. And moments later I am slipping behind the black emergence of Son of Sorrows. He glares at Ralph.

"Grandad Nankavelle!" The two words tumble from his mouth like poison arrows. He doesn't see Ralph. He sees my grandfather cleaning the lenses of the spectacles. "The father and grandfather are both the fucking same! Mean old bastards! Do you have any idea what I had to fucking put up with when the father took me to the grandparents'?"

"No, you tell me." Ralph is about to say more but he's cut short by Son of Sorrows' verbal outrage.

"Budding prostitutes, my fuckin' arse! Cassandra and Nicole were only normal teenagers. Loveless old bastard. The father was always calling Nicole awful names. And the grandparents turned up at No-Exit Street after the parents had moved out of the house . . ."

"Your parents left the house you were living in?" Ralph studies the anger in Son of Sorows' face. "How old were you?"

"Let's fucking say that a part of me was twelve years old when they left. The brother looked after us."

"Us?" Ralph is perplexed. (Or is he?)

"Yeah, fuck — us! Nicole, Peter, Cassandra and part of me."

Ralph breathes a sigh for a moment. "What part of you?"

"Nankavelle. Me, Nankavelle. Okay!"

— Matthew Nankavelle, I'm saving your fucking arse here. You'd better not talk about the Others!

— He knows about you, Son of Sorrows. Ralph is pretty clued-up.

— Just don't get me in the shit. Why the fuck do I come here! . . .

My internal dialogue with him comes to an abrupt halt as I'm jolted back into Ralph's world by a swift but gentle kick on the foot. "Talk to me."

I get the idea that Ralph wants Son of Sorrows to continue talking about my father and grandfather, so I instead fill in the details, nervously. "My grandparents came to visit after Mum and Dad had gone. They were concerned about the house being in such a mess. Fuck, it was a dump! Cassandra and Nicole were outside getting onto their boyfriends' motorbikes. Grandad said, 'Will you look at that — budding prostitutes, just like their mother!' He made the remark just because the girls were wearing mini skirts."

Ralph asks, "At what point did your parents leave you in your brother's care?"

"A year after their marriage broke up. Peter was fifteen. He had a girlfriend and baby. I hated living there."

"Were you frightened?" My therapist looks at me wet eyed. I'm feeling choked up too, knowing that what I am telling Ralph is reaching him, it's something he can understand and relate to. I'm aware that not only my own pain but also Son of Sorrows' rage has an effect on him to some degree. Now I'm aware again of the fear evoked by Ralph's simple act of putting on his glasses. It reminds me of my grandfather, and that fear is of being misunderstood.

I don't have a chance to answer my therapist's question. The Mad-Child appears. He's like a cat on a hot tin roof. Nervous, idiotic, living in a perpetual state of terror, a lost boy who won't grow up. I'm in limbo between him and Son of Sorrows whom I can hear cursing from the dark recesses of my being.

— Look out, here comes the Illiterate Fool. Better keep your mouth shut, Fuck Brain!

The Mad-Child squirms in his seat and giggles nervously.

t h i r t y

THE BODY SPEAKS:

When some of the Others feel shame in a public place, muscle tone is diminished and The Mind affected also. The cheeks flush and Nankavelle feels stupefied, almost as if drunk. To escape social humiliation he must find the nearest exit, but to leave a crowded room is a real ordeal when the legs drag, the eyes are so sightless that the Mad-Child walks into doors, windows and occasionally the wall. The heart rate soars, bringing numbness to the face, dizziness and nausea too. As the fingers feel their way along the wall, desperately in search of a way out, onlookers find it amusing. Speech becomes slurred as Nankavelle says in despair, "Where's the door?" The Body is malfunctioning under the strain of it all. Such anxiety is paralysing and to observers it appears that Nankavelle is suffering cerebral palsy. Shame is truly crippling.

THE ABSOLUTE END of the line. Zero. Infinity, the land of nothingness. I can no longer fight. Son of Sorrows has kicked the guts out of me. This is the vanishing point where I concede defeat — death of my mind, an orphan cast out of his own flesh.

My telephone calls to Ralph are frequent, in the middle of the night. My confusing messages are left on his answer-phone by the dozens. At the forefront of my mind I have a blurry recollection of my therapist saying, "I'm your life-line. Call when you need to. You'll be feeling quite raw now."

What little hope of reality I am grasping for is not my own but Ralph's, because I can't see any tomorrow to hang onto. I can at least take hold of my therapist's hand. Like someone deaf and dumb and blind, I clutch at whatever portion of reality he offers. This is an experience I'll never forget. For the first time in all my life I've reached a stage where somebody else, outside of myself, has to steer the ship. Ralph at the helm is very loving and I'm forced to put aside any fears, to trust him completely. There are times when I can't feel Ralph there but I'm to realise many years later that it is the Mad-Child he so lovingly guides.

On rare occasions I leave the flat. I spend days and nights in and out of bed, sitting at my desk in the corner of the bedroom, typing my own first novel. Trevor Daniels oversees this writing process. After numerous black-outs I find his edited version, criss-crossed and punctuated with a red biro, beside the Olivetti.

Other selves are living through me constantly. My place amidst this psychic anarchy is to float about in a dark, clammy state of suspension within the abyss.

When I do surface, it is to feed the stomach: cold baked beans, dry bread, and countless cups of black sugarless tea. I've lost touch with The Body. It has betrayed me, so why bother caring for it? To see myself in the bathroom mirror is to look into teary eyes surrounded by dark racoon circles. I study the reflection, trying to believe that the person I see is a dead or dying shell with the vague title of "Me".

As I can't bear to leave the flat, it is Trevor Daniels who scoots about the local mall, buying groceries and paying enormously high power bills (thanks to the tiny hot water cylinder by the bath, forever boiling). His long hair, tied with a red elastic band, is soaking by the time I reappear, standing on the side doorstep with a key in my hand. Cold rainwater drips down the back of my neck as I anxiously ask him, Where have we been? It dawns on me that a heavy shopping bag is weighing down my right hand. I slip the key in the lock, pull the door shut behind me and rifle through the contents of the bag. Beef steak? But why buy such a large amount?

— We have a visitor for tea . . . But he says no more.

As it turns out I never find out exactly who comes to tea. I'm suddenly alone very late at night. The house has an after-smell of hearty casserole and there are two dirty plates in the kitchen sink. I have vague memories of Russell laughing with somebody.

— I thought you'd gone, forever. Bastard! You've been having sex. Who with?

He chooses not to answer my question, so I play detective: no wet patches on the sheets, no pubic hair around the toilet bowl, no faded trace of after-shave on the pillows. So who? Perhaps I'll never know.

For someone who's at the end of the line, I fail to comprehend just how many lives I am living. And why should I care? Wasn't it Son of

Sorrows who said, None of us need you, you're not important now! — and other cruel threats, wishing me to die. Yeah, I am dying alright because I'm certainly not living, and what hurts the most is that I'm the one who's stopping me. I've begun to wish death upon myself. It doesn't occur to me that I'm suffering from severe depression.

Ralph has wisened up to the Others. He knows they're ruling my life, using my airtime. What fragmented moments he has with me are to smile and say, "It does get better."

How can I have faith in this therapist? He sees perhaps eight of us while in fact there are thirty-eight. The Others won't come forward. Ralph is a liability to their continued existence. An awakening and gradual fusing of all the selves could mean their eventual death. They have survived for so long now, why kill them with integration? Theirs is the right to live.

I pussyfoot around the truth, avoid Ralph's digging and prodding to reveal the possible existence of others. The fear I have is that he'll stamp in red ink and bold letters across my brow: INSANE! And then the whole bloody routine will repeat itself: white coats, pink rooms, and a shot in the bum of anti-schizophrenia medication. Who needs that all over again? I don't.

It is a deft presumption on my part that Ralph only sees the Others who are lively, confident, gutsy — therefore seeing a happy healthy person. When observing me through Trevor Daniels, Son of Sorrows and the more dominant selves, Ralph is actually seeing what has become of me: vitality-gusto rather than the sadly depleted, what-is-left-of-me.

So . . . this is it. Time to close shop. I, the coward, want to quit, give way, sink.

But just as I'm about to will myself into a mental institution, the most incredible miracle occurs. Daniel, the voice of hope. He comes at the point where I've been reduced to a quivering wreck because Son of Sorrows has been continually tormenting me. I've even started to pray, Lord Jesus, take me now, with a carving knife in one hand and Son of Sorrows screaming in my head, — Across the artery!

At that precise moment Daniel, God-sent, speaks within me:

— Matthew? Don't listen to him. I'm here to help you.

ANOTHER ONE? ANOTHER person inside me? Surely it isn't possible for there to be one more? This is like starring in a never-ending horror movie where the main character finds his body is invaded by other entities. What next? Maybe I'll wake up in a church with a priest throwing holy water at me, my head rotating a full three hundred and sixty degrees, masturbating with a crucifix, snarling wicked profanities.

I know what. I'll block this new self out. All of them can be kept a secret. Nobody need ever know.

I am kidding myself — one more white lie to dodge the truth.

— What about Ralph?

— Fourteen, you turn up at the oddest times. Go away!

My head is silent once more. I'm allowed some breathing space. I need this time to take stock of my life, plan a roadway out of this absurdness. I must be acting, surely? A bored twenty two year old who's seeking attention, secretly dramatising quirky thoughts, living out fantasies of being other selves. An impostor (or impostors). Yes, I've made all this up, telling lies to my therapist. Now I'll stop being so immature, act my age, cancel therapy, get a job, live a real life . . .

— You must not fight this, that loving voice of Daniel warns.

I'm walking around my living room, speaking my thoughts aloud, pinching my forearm, saying, "You're not real. This is a lie!" I'm desperately trying to convince myself that the past few years, all these strange postures, the foreign thought patterns, other voices using my vocal chords and mouth, are all my imagination. "Nothing but my imagination . . ."

But the voice speaks calmly within. I feel his presence as truth and wholesomeness, washing through me. I can relax with the sound of his voice which is clear, warm, soothing. He's saying, — Matthew . . . you must listen to me. You have little choice but to believe in us.

I'm worried, worse than usual, because a new voice is one more complication to an already complex situation. Now I really am losing it, pacing the room with a stupid, violent urge to bust up the furniture. "I need a doctor to jab me with a needleful of . . . anything!"

Tears stream down my face and I'm fearful that when the next blackout comes I'll not only disappear into the abyss but I won't come back. I'm speaking aloud to these people who are conversing inside me, using the inside of my head like a party line.

"I want to scream. Do you all hear me? I want to open my mouth and scream until I can't scream any more! We are all so real . . ." Oh my God! We? We? Now I've said it . . . We!

— We all have to get along together because we all share the same space. Daniel is speaking softly, mediating to a lost cause of peace.

— But this is my body . . .

— Agreed. But, Matthew, you don't have much choice. I can help you, and the Others. Some of the Others *will* help you . . .

NEVER MIND EXACTLY *who I am. The name is Daniel. Soon you'll be able to understand my function within the abyss.*

My entry into that dark warm place is only brief, to nurture "It", the Child, before standing guard again outside the Memory Door.

Perhaps, after all, I should tell you who I am and why I'm here. How harmful can such honesty be? You may look into Nankavelle's face but you're unaware that ten centimetres behind the eyes is where I reside — and behind me is the fragmented child.

You probably want to know how old am I? What my mannerisms are? Like Ralph the therapist, you probably presume that I'll surface one day — real, three-dimensional. I had better disappoint you — gently. While I am a person (as such) my voice never expresses itself via Matthew's lips. It is impossible, too, for me to surface in his body. Remember, I dwell within; to desert my post, to leave "It" the Child alone, even for several seconds, could have dire consequences. Son of Sorrows hates "It" — and why? Because "It", as you now understand, is the core of our being; with "It" are the scourge marks of hell and cruelty, wounds so deep that the poor Child barely manages to remain alive. Hypothetically speaking, then, the destruction of "It" would upset the balance between all the selves. The therapist could get to the core of our being and find nothing.

My manifestation came about when "It" and Matthew Nankavelle were very young. What the Child saw with his eyes and felt with his body, years ago in No-Exit Street, was enough to cause his disintegration. Do you know what happens to a person when their inner self is partially destroyed or taken away? Simply, I'll tell you. Try driving a car with no motor. There may be a new coat of paint, new chrome window wipers, even a total refurbishment, but do these things have the power to activate the vehicle?

Supposing the therapist gets to "It"? What then? I'll explain. A vacuum would be created. All the Others would be sucked into it, the mind emptied of all its content. Soul death. A person with no mind, emotions drained dry; memory storage deleted — past, present, and future. The equivalent of being comatose, but without unconscious awareness of the physical realm. Dead, I tell you.

Ralph is an utterly wonderful man but I will not allow him longer than even two minutes' audience with "It". He believes, like many psychologists, that when the soul is emptied it can be re-educated, refilled with new language, emotions, responses — a rebuilt interior.

Kind, loving Ralph! Matthew adores him, emulates him, but this is not good enough reason to let the Child stay surfaced. This is not a matter of mistrust — though I'm sure Ralph perceives it to be. No, absolutely not! This is protection of sacred territory. One accidental slip and the Child could be crushed — probably forever. So, yes, while I do permit the therapist precious time with "It", there are barely enough moments for this to be of therapeutic value.

Ralph understands that all of Us are not only "selves" but also a process. Our process is to live and fade away to nothing, our last nourishing breaths seeping through the walls of the abyss and thus feeding the Child. Whether "It" will grow with time is debatable. His choice, at present, is to sleep. The fear within the Child is enormous. To gently pat his arm would cause a crumbling of all progress made. I say leave "It" alone — his strength shall be our reservoir.

I had better tell you about Matthew Nankavelle now:

He is a sensitive man who is, at last, putting that ugly hospital diagnosis, and the stigma attached, behind him. He's a worry-wart, often too honest for his own good — a phobic, delicate and traumatised person. Lately he has been awakening to my reality, beginning to realise that I alone can help him through these darkened times.

How well he listens to me! When he's on the edge of his own peculiar form of madness — an obsessive fear, really, of being violated or murdered — I talk within his mind, calming him, carrying him through public life when he is too frail to stand tall.

What is important is that I, only I, can operate the Memory Door.

Symbolically, it is the gateway to the subconscious — to that filthy place, to hell, where the past slithers about and is remembered, though is often too painful for him to comprehend. Should he remember something which is detrimental to his emotional well-being, I must intercept that memory and refile it back behind the Memory Door. I can also call up childhood memories at random, edit them and present them in censored form so he'll cope with their recall.

But I can do much more. When the Others are fearful in a public place or situation, I talk them through it. When Matthew is too anxious about leaving the familiarity of Sherbourne Street I direct him through the heavy traffic and busy suburban streets. I dictate to him during his social predicaments and guide him through simple problem solving. More importantly, I hold Son of Sorrows at arm's length, away from all the Others.

I also have the power to erase thought processes, and recall — via the Others — lost segments of time. Best of all, I oversee Matthew Daniels, Trevor Daniels and Alex Daniels in all their writing endeavours. I have assigned myself this dominion over all creative energy because Matthew Nankavelle was ostracised in childhood for being a "dreamer". In time, all of us will become less distinct, meld together, and have little reason for hiding away from society. If you only knew how talented a man Matthew Nankavelle is — by way of the Daniels selves he will accomplish many things. No, I am not being prophetic, I am merely telling you from the heart, from the centre of this life meshed over with varied levels of consciousness: the pen will be his greatest success.

I am soaking up information, creating learning curves, refashioning The Mind. Matthew will fly one day and carry my name while I and the Others will all be gone.

See, the life history within each of us is not so much a helping hand out of a traumatic past: all that pain is our liberation! We need Nankavelle as much as he needs us.

thirtyone

THE EASIEST WAY to disable a person is through fear. Once you've discovered someone's worst fear, then you have them, by playing on that fear itself. Turn out the lights on the one who is scared of the dark. Walk away from the one who is frightened of abandonment. And so on.

To disable can mean accelerating someone's heartbeat, pushing them to the point of hysteria, and if you're cruel enough, throwing them over the edge.

Terrorised people will do anything under the dominant reign of fear. Once they're pushed over the brink these people can become robots, saying and doing anything you want them to — behaving in a way which is totally out of character, committing acts they'd normally never do if they were otherwise unafraid.

Fear is fear. Terror is something else. It creates a mental cot-case, a puppet on a string, the defiance of all logic: I'm ordering you! Jump off that cliff, now! The puppet has no speech, no mind, little resistance at this point: Before I jump, do you want my body to smash on the rocks below? He's like a child beckoned to an adult's knee: Come, give Uncle a kiss goodnight. And while the puppet's mouth says, Sure! the eyes say, What will it be, Uncle? Hand job? . . . Oral?

I think you get the picture.

But beware the double-edged sword. One side of the victim is black, with brain-dead eyes, robotic; the opposite side is a time bomb ticking away, the I'll-Kill-You-Later syndrome. Indescribable fear breeds a potent form of rage: Enjoy me . . . but Son of Sorrows will kill you later.

And now, enter the demon of seduction: Here I am, wide-eyed, flirtatious, the Woman who deludes herself into thinking she's been untouched, virginal. Kiss, kiss . . .

If I could hold you
In my arms,
I'd sweat liquid nitrogen —
And freeze your goddamned heart.

MY FAVOURITE HIDING place was in the shoe cupboard in the long hallway, just beside the front door. Can't find me! There's a full-length curtain across the front of the cupboard and I'm hiding behind an oilskin coat; standing inside a cardboard box with many, many shoes around me.

"Fe Fi Fo Fum, I smell the blood of an Englishman." My father is stomping his feet all the way down the hall.

Giant's coming! He's coming! If only I could melt into the back of the closet wall. He's gunna get me! I pretend, while holding my breath, that I'm dead, because dead boys can't be haunted by giants. My little heart is hammering away inside my chest. My mouth is dry and I'm frozen into a standing position behind the coat. Don' make a sound!

— Won't, I won't . . .

— Ssh, no breath.

— I dead, I dead. Can'ts catch me.

— Ssh, quiet. Giant's coming. Be here soon . . .

The heart-stopping moment arrives. My father is growling like a wild animal right outside the shoe cupboard. A prickling sensation twists upward along my spine to the back of my neck. I feel dizzy and weak, desperately trying to convince myself that I've died. Don' scream. You must be quiet.

The tension is electrifying. I'm going to be hauled out of the cupboard. My limbs will be torn off by the hungry giant and I will be chewed up by gnashing teeth, my bones spat out . . .

— God! You help? You, God, Help?

— God's not's here. In heaven, boy!

The giant is breathing heavily now. His breath is rasping and I imagine his eyes to be cruel yellow slits of rage.

— He's gunna eat me!

— Ssh, stands still, boy!

A hand comes through the curtain. I wish I was dead. The heavy fingers press into the oilskin coat. I dead, I dead! I want to go to the toilet badly. I want the giant to go away. I want the lights to be turned on again.

I'm nothing any more. I have no pulse rate or heartbeat. Nothing exists. My brain has liquefied, it's jelly. I'm emotionless, wooden-faced, babbling and raving. I'm thick and stupid and flighty. Everything scares me. Later, in years to come, Ralph will give me a name: the Village Idiot. The boy inside the shoe cupboard with me will forever be unidentified. Unnamed.

I'VE NEVER BEEN *lucky enough to have a name. And I'm too fragile, too fragmented to surface for lengthy amounts of time outside of the abyss.*

My thoughts and emotions are primitive. The basic function of my existence is to snatch up food, eat, and scream for fear of being hungry. To slip from my place of perpetual sleep is like being aborted: I'm blinded by daylight, my body hurts and all I can feel is the fear of possible human touch. I have no recognition of ever being human.

Nobody outside of The Body can touch or hold me in their arms because I vomit and rock my body in an up-and-down motion. Ralph tells Nankavelle that I will be human one day soon.

Nankavelle refers to me as "It". That's because he can't think of me as human.

At all hours of day and night another stands before me, keeping watch: his guarding of my darkened, warm chamber is the only reason I can actually sleep. I don't know his name but every now and then tension and emotion leak through the tunnel to me when my guard is under attack.

I am very important and must never die. I will keep existing, often unconsciously, otherwise Matthew Nankavelle has no beginning. I am the first self, the Original Child. Without me all their lives would have never begun.

I was a whole person very many years ago.

MUM AND DAD have no religious beliefs. Dad is highly amused by what he calls "Bible Bashers" who knock on our front door. Mormons on bikes, Jehovah's Witnesses. Dad says that these people are "mental".

I believe in Jesus. He loves me. The Sunday School teacher said so. I sin a lot. I swear, fly into dizzying heights of black anger. I even stole an eighty-cent book about cats from a bookshop. I was out of pocket money. Mother's Day was looming closer and I really wanted to buy Mum a gift. She doesn't like flowers and I'm tired of making cards.

After stealing the book from the shop in Otahuhu I scurry along the footpath. My heart is pounding and I'm feeling guilty and afraid for what I've just done.

I'm in trouble. The police are going to come to our house in a black car. I'm going to jail now. I arrive home feeling like I'm balanced on a tightrope, waiting, fretting, worrying. I'm gunna go where the bad kids go. God won't love me any more. My fear snowballs. I'll only be fed bread and water!

I give Mum her gift. She cuddles me and kisses my soft nine-year-old cheek. I peer out the kitchen window. They're coming soon! Every car that drives into No-Exit Street has me burning with fear. The black police car is here. I'll hide from them.

Jesus loves all the children of the world. He loves everybody, even sinners. His eyes are green and God makes it rain all day because I've made him sad. God will be angry now — I didn't mean to steal the book! Jesus wears long dresses with sandals, and he's heartbroken because everyone on earth is doing wrong. God the Father is a bad-tempered, horrible, mean old man. He never shaves off his long white beard and he's a thousand years old. Nana is too! He wears a starched white robe and sits on a golden chair. When God the Father is angry he makes thunder and lightning. The kids in our street say that God is throwing chairs around in heaven and that's what the noise is. God can do anything because he's the boss of our world.

I've been thinking: "There's gold at the end of the rainbow. We could catch a bus there and be rich."

"There's no gold at the rainbow's end," said a girl in No-Exit Street.

"There is . . . it's in a witch's pot!"

"Is not!" Karen said.

"There is!" I stated quite matter-of-factly. But somehow I never made it to the pot of gold. I was too busy playing childhood games, skipping ropes and singing silly ditties:

> My mummy she told me to open the door
> But I didn't want to . . .
> I opened the door and he fell through the floor,
> That crazy man from China . . .

ON AN OVERCAST Thursday afternoon in 1990 I board the Big Red bus to Cathedral Square before visiting my sister Nicole. Gloom and loneliness weigh heavily upon my shoulders. I speak to nobody on board the bus, just stare out the window, wishing that I was somewhere else.

It's Nicole's birthday and I walk through Whitcoulls Arcade in search of a gift for my sister. After browsing for several minutes I come upon a sale table of desktop lamps. Just the thing! With the wrapped lamp under my arm I amble, head down, for the Dallington bus stop, chain smoke for twenty minutes until the bus pulls up, and then journey to my sister's flat thinking of nothing but my loneliness.

She greets me at the door with a huge hug and smile. "Come in," she invites. "You want a cuppa?" Seated on the couch we exchange news. I feel awful that I have very little of interest to offer. I've written another chapter of my novel, on Tuesday I went down to the local fruit shop and visited my new doctor. My reclusive lifestyle doesn't allow for anything outside the mundane.

Nicole loves the lamp. She coos and fusses about the room, trying the lamp out in different positions — behind the TV, on the mantelpiece. "I like the colour. I'll put it on the computer desk." She can see how unhappy I am, though we giggle over the antics of her two kittens roughing and tumbling under the rug in her kitchen. Chester the cat hides under the mat, his wide yellow eyes like saucers. "Moray eel eyes," comments Nicole which greatly amuses me. It perks me up for a short while.

I'm not in the mood for lengthy conversation that day, but I notice that my sister often stops in the middle of her chatter to look at me with a loving twinkle in her eyes. "You're my favourite brother!" she beams. I'm touched by this but too wrapped up in my private thoughts to acknowledge her affections. I feel that she is just trying to cheer me up. While struggling to keep my end of the conversation my heart goes out to Nicole: I love you, too. But I can't say it.

AFTER WAVING GOODBYE to Nicole I climb onto the Big Red back to town. I'm full of guilt that I was unable to express my feelings for her — God knows, I've loved her very deeply since my earliest living memory. She's always been there. We've felt each other's pain through the rollercoaster ride of our bizarre childhood.

While riding on that bus, tears well up in my eyes. I begin to pray to God, Please, God, I can't stand this loneliness any longer. Why do I have to be gay? I'll never have a happy fulfilled life without the love of another of my own sex. Can't you break the rules for me, let me meet another gay man, let me love him and let him love me? Don't tell me physical love between men is wrong. Help me, God. I've got to share my life with someone like myself.

In a moment of emotional turmoil the content of the prayer changes dramatically. I pour out my troubles to my Maker, determined that he hear my voice: Why, God? Why am I alone? I've heard it said that some people find comfort in You, but that's not enough for me. Quite honestly I think Your rules on homosexuality stink! You and the bloody churches expect me to be alone and celibate. Damn it, God, I can't accept that. My bitterness reaches its peak as the bus eases up to the kerb and stops in Cathedral Square: All that shit about love and happiness in You. I'm telling you, God, much more loneliness and I'll kill myself. The end to my one-way dialogue with the Almighty is as unorthodox as the prayer itself; there is no "Amen", only a cry of despair: You're not fucking real anyway, God!

The double doors at the back of the Big Red swing open. I stomp down the steps. As I hurry along Colombo Street, feeling really low, I peek into the gay café where I used to go, just for old time's sake. There are new owners now and the café has been refurbished with wooden chairs, varnished tables, and ghastly chequered tablecloths. The place is empty.

Inside five minutes I arrive at the Cranford Street bus stop where I go to check the timetable. Preoccupied with my own thoughts, I don't even see the outstretched legs of a man who's sitting at the end of the glass bus shelter. I trip over his feet. Embarrassed, I apologise and steal a sidelong glance at him. He's bundled up in a thick nylon jacket, looks handsome and seems like he'd be a nice fellow to talk to. Damn it, I'm lonely!

"Next bus isn't too far away," I say tentatively as I sit down next to him. "Have you got the time on you?" What a hunk!

"Yeah," says the man, his hazel eyes glinting, inviting. "Ten to four. Sorry about leaving my legs out so far. I didn't mean to trip you up."

"Don't worry about it. It was my fault, I wasn't watching where I was going." I study the man's face briefly and feel a rush of blood to my groin. Before a sexual fantasy can take over I quickly engage my mind in a different direction. I mention the recent A & P Show Week procession through the city and we talk about the West Coast where the man has stayed near a magical settlement called Denniston. I ask him, "What do you do for a job?"

"I'm a copywriter for an advertising agency," he replies, smiling.

"Really? I write too. I'm working on a novel at the moment."

"We should get together and talk some time. It's not often I meet another writer."

We climb onto the same bus and get off at the same stop in St Albans. I turn eastward to my flat in Sherbourne Street, he heads westward to his rental house, but not before we quickly exchange addresses and phone numbers. I don't expect I'll ever hear from him again. But I do.

Little do I realise it, but I'm on the threshold of a new beginning.

Over the next three years I will say goodbye, one by one, to most of the thirty-eight selves who now populate my inner world. I will start to meet new people, make new friends and live in the outer world again. Of course, the half-a-lifetime swallowed up in the abyss can never be reclaimed. Is there any way I can make up for what's been lost? Maybe not, but I'll have a damned good job trying!

The Mind and Body which divided into many selves are about to see the return of the stranger who left home around age eleven.

That stranger is . . . me.

And the life which is about to begin is mine.

Mine alone.

Almost.

EPILOGUE

*T*HAT GENTLE-EYED MAN I met at the bus stop not only called into my Sherbourne Street home for coffee — he stayed and we have been lovers for almost seven years now. Chris is my closest friend, a fellow writer, and we share the same passion for most forms of art, music, adventurous (healthy) food — and of course, we are people mad.

While, in the past, our commitment to each other has raised a few eyebrows, these days we are well received by our families and friends, even admired. Some say, "Your relationship is better than a lot of heterosexual ones." However, we've travelled darker roads to get to our present destination, with wounds and bruising in the process because of our mutually impulsive natures. In the early stages, when I was at the mercy of other selves, I inevitably 'switched' on numerous occasions. This caused ruptures in our communications. At times I frightened Chris with the many crises arising from having multiple personalities, and to complicate an already troubled relationship, he was experiencing severe depression, coming to terms with his long-denied orientation. Thankfully, our love for each other was the strong thread that bound us together through the many storms, though admittedly that thread was tested to breaking strain. In 1991 we sought couples counselling and individual therapy to bridge the rift of hurts, misunderstanding and resentment that lay between us.

During the early days of our life together I retreated from society and continued to write, haphazardly scrawling page after page of terrible short stories and one unfinished novel. Over a three-year period Chris began to distance himself from advertising writing and to concentrate on adult fiction, children's stories and illustrating.

My most potent self-discovery was, one morning, to hear the voice of Matthew Daniels greeting me for the first time. For some weeks I'd been baffled to find pages of appealing text mysteriously turning up beside my typewriter. They impressed me deeply but, naturally, I thought, No way did I write those! That story is too good to be mine anyway. It was a sudden transition from my own spare narrative to Matthew Daniels' more crackling style, so I could see no connection. When I awoke that morning, finding myself seated at the kitchen table with a story typed up before me, and Matthew Daniels saying, "We are good writers!" I immediately understood what had been happening. His pen was in my hand and I was wearing his tweed sportscoat. His voice moved me and I warmed to his presence, his humour and of course, his go-get-'em attitude. Matthew Daniels became so strong a force in my life that I entered the abyss once again, not surfacing for great lengths of time. After a name change by deed poll was officiated, my partner Chris continued to love a man who wasn't me any more.

Enter, the cast: the Mad-Child, Russell, Trouble, Terry, Speed, the Illiterate One, Night-eyes, Trevor Daniels, the Kiwi Male, Cody, the Adolescent, the Woman, Thomas the Poet, Son of Sorrows and the whole host of other selves . . .

For three years these selves would confuse my partner, driving him to distraction with their conflicting forms of behaviour, their different mannerisms, and their thoughts quite foreign to my own. Over the years Chris has learned to accept the surfacing of other selves. This was often an ugly and anxious encounter for him to endure, and even today I still wonder why he chose to remain in our relationship. (He says he believed in me. He felt that the beautiful person he'd first glimpsed and fallen in love with was still there, somewhere, and would re-emerge. He was prepared to wait, convinced that time would eventually heal much of my pain, restoring what had been depleted by fragmentation.)

What now is a blessing from some higher power is that my life and Chris's life — our lives together — have improved beyond expectation and we're able to emotionally support and inspire each other in our publishing careers. Since 1995 I've had a children's book published which my partner illustrated, I've had other small successes with non-fiction articles and poetry, and my desk is cluttered with incompleted texts and plots for future novels. Chris has illustrated another children's book for a Wellington publisher, had short fiction published in the School Journal and has three-quarters finished his first novel. We live in a bungalow surrounded by trees, in our favourite Christchurch suburb of St Albans, with one black cat called Sinbad and three aquarium fish, Monty, Finn 1 and

Finn 2. Soon we will celebrate our seventh year together as we continue to encourage each other in our mutual obsession of writing and reading New Zealand fiction.

IT IS TRUE that I'm not always the person who fell in love with Chris. To my knowledge there are fifteen selves who still exist. Their surfacing, on rare occasions nowadays, creates in me a minimal amount of anxiety. There is one self I've yet to meet who is very evasive. I know that his existence is genuine because whenever he appears everything of importance to me disappears, is turned upside down or is destroyed. The evidence he leaves is like a calling card which says, "Ha ha, I'm here but you will never find me!" Somehow I erase all memory of his having surfaced.

What is vital is that I keep attending therapy each fortnight. I have a great need to build the confidence of four selves who are present and central to my life right now.

In retrospect, the diagnosis of schizophrenia has become something to laugh about. It is virtually past history in 1997. I'm left with a sincere wish that medical practitioners think carefully before placing such a heavy label upon any young person. Continued moral support comes from my GP and therapist, both down-to-earth men who encourage me in my writing. Their viewpoint is that the "psychoses" I've experienced have involved great historical recall: unresolved childhood conflicts which unfortunately manifest (though rarely) as a garbled mass of past and present memories. These "psychoses" are the products of the Mad-Child's traumatic background. One day I'll again confirm that child's presence, letting him out to exclaim to myself, "See, this child's mess is part of my hidden compartmentalised childhood, and he's Nankavelle 3."

AS YOU'VE SEEN recreated in this account, Multiple Personality Disorder is a very real and unusual division of the mind. Some psychiatrists reject the idea that a cluster of individual personalities can simultaneously exist within one mind. What can I say? Perhaps the possibility of MPD may seem not only absurd but fantastic because the media and American television dramas have portrayed this unique life force in a simplified form, diluting it down to another freak-show sensation or a psychopathic tragedy.

For myself, being divided is not a drama, nor is it a deliberate form of histrionic self-expressionism. It is real, though as plain and ordinary as toast.

Of the sceptics of MPD, I can only ask: Is there any other logical explanation?

As I MENTIONED at the beginning, I've been in private therapy for eleven years now. To meet me you'd probably conclude that I'm a level-headed and semi-confident man. That's because, over recent years of growing self-awareness, I've designed a system of preventing most of the remaining Others from surfacing. Nevertheless, I'm often expressing their thoughts — with my own voice. I can edit them out, and camouflage them with my own behavioural patterns. From time to time this is recognised by the casual comment, "Matthew's not quite himself."

Ah, yes, *we are all here* in limbo . . . just below the surface!

There are further years of therapy ahead of me, but this thing called "My Life" is stabilising. And where do I go from here? I'll get a part-time job; I'll keep on with my greatest passion which is, of course, writing. Simply put, I'll laugh and love and live — no matter who from within claims a portion of my time.

POSTSCRIPT

*T*HE BULK OF this manuscript was written via the Daniels self — recalled and dictated from within the abyss by myself, Nankavelle. However, four months ago, during November 1996, all that remains of the person who is Matthew Daniels was reabsorbed into the dark place. Since then I have been in dialogue with him. It has been acknowledged between the two of us that I'll retain the name of Matthew Daniels despite his eventual self-disintegration.

Matthew Nankavelle 1
Matthew Nankavelle 2
as Matthew Daniels
1 MARCH 1997